What people are saying about …

"Now more than ever it's important to know what you believe and why you believe it. As a Christian in an increasingly skeptical world, we must do more than tell people what the Bible teaches; we must help them understand why they can trust what it says about Jesus. Are you ready to make the case? *Forensic Faith* will help you develop a faith that's dedicated, inquisitive, and prepared to answer the tough questions."

Andy Stanley, senior pastor of North Point
Community Church, Alpharetta, Georgia

"Today, too many evangelical Christians would rather 'feel' their faith than actually understand and defend it. With biblical precision, solid evidence and masterful reasoning, J. Warner Wallace challenges believers to both embrace and make a thoughtful and intellectually robust case for historic Christianity. *Forensic Faith* is exactly what the church needs today!"

Janet Mefferd, nationally syndicated Christian radio
personality and host of *Janet Mefferd Today*

"Charles Malik, famed ambassador to the US, rightly quipped, 'If you win the whole world and lose the mind of the world, you will soon discover that you have not won the world. Indeed, it may turn out that you have actually lost the world.' In *Forensic Faith*, Christian apologist J. Warner Wallace underscores the danger of anti-intellectualism and equips you to do something about it."

Hank Hanegraaff, host of the *Bible Answer Man* broadcast,
bestselling author, and president of the Christian Research Institute

"J. Warner Wallace's *Forensic Faith* completes the trilogy of wonderful books making the evidentiary case for the historicity and veracity of the Christian faith in language that twenty-first-century Americans can clearly and readily understand. I have seldom seen an approach to verifying the truth claims of the Christian faith that is more effective than the one taken by 'God's police detective,' J. Warner Wallace. Buy two copies of this book. Read one and keep it, and share one with a lost friend."

Dr. Richard Land, president of Southern Evangelical Seminary

"Few professions better prepare a person to follow the evidence than being a detective. And few detectives are better prepared Christians to be apologists than J. Warner Wallace. This book is a classic in how to be a more effective defender of the Christian faith. I highly recommend it for every Christian, even for those who have given no thought to being an apologist."

Dr. Norm Geisler, chancellor of Veritas Evangelical Seminary and author of over one hundred books, including *Conversational Evangelism*

"Unless you're one of the three people in America who believe the church is successfully making disciples and winning over the culture, *Forensic Faith* is a book that you must read and heed NOW! Detective Wallace shows you how to make a persuasive case for Christianity and why it's absolutely necessary to do so. The third book in a brilliant series (*Cold-Case Christianity, God's Crime Scene*), *Forensic Faith* is not only insightful and practical, it is beautifully illustrated. So join the growing movement of case makers to help advance God's kingdom by putting this book into practice NOW!"

Dr. Frank Turek, Christian apologist, president of CrossExamined Ministries, and author of *I Don't Have Enough Faith to Be an Atheist* and *Stealing from God*

"J. Warner Wallace has done us all a service with *Forensic Faith*. In these pages, Jim not only makes a great case for the importance of apologetics but also gives us a thorough and thoughtful method for how to use apologetics in discussing the credibility of the Christian faith. As a trained trial attorney and evangelist, I highly recommend *Forensic Faith*."

Abdu Murray, North American director of Ravi Zacharias International Ministries and author of *Grand Central Question*

"Perhaps, more today than ever, Christians need to be able to defend what they believe and why they believe it, and to do so with passion and proof. In this book, J. Warner Wallace reminds us that the truth is fearless and so should be every true believer."

Jack Hibbs, senior pastor of Calvary Chapel Chino
Hills and host of *Real Life with Jack Hibbs*

"Whether you are an individual looking for where to start answering doubts about Christianity or you are a church community looking to better train and equip your people, *Forensic Faith* is the practical guide you need. J. Warner Wallace has brought together his intriguing detective stories with practical help for the beginning case maker. It's like a reader 'ride-along' in a police cruiser, learning the ropes on how to thoughtfully investigate the truth."

Mary Jo Sharp, assistant professor of apologetics, Houston
Baptist University, and author of *Resilient Faith* and *Why
Do You Believe That? A Faith Conversation*

"'What is truth?' Pontius Pilate's question reverberates through the ages to our own skeptical day. J. Warner Wallace challenges you to answer the Pilates of your day with Jesus's words 'I have come into the world to bear witness to the truth,' and then he equips you to make the case for that truth. More than anyone I have read, Jim trains you to think, prepares you to practice, and encourages you to step out with *Forensic Faith*."

Bill Parkinson, founding and "Sageworks" pastor of
Fellowship Bible Church, Little Rock, Arkansas

"This book connects. It is one of the most accessible books addressing the foundational issues in apologetics I have ever seen. Superb material—that every Christian student and leader needs to master—presented in a way that is enormously thoughtful and engaging. My hope is that churches around the globe read it, study it, and apply it. It will turn the church, and then the world, upside down."

Craig J. Hazen, PhD, founder and director of the Graduate Program
in Christian apologetics and author of *Five Sacred Crossings*

"Most apologetics texts introduce the major evidences favoring Christianity. Having completed that task already in two previous volumes, J. Warner Wallace's third book in his trilogy, *Forensic Faith*, is one of only a handful of books that wades into the turbulent waters among the sharks and shows readers how actually to apply the evidences. And why not? As a cold-case homicide detective in Los Angeles for many years and a passionate atheist as well, Jim's job was to emphasize real-life applications of evidence in the toughest situations. But while applying the same rules used in solving murders, he realized after a long search that Christianity was absolutely true! Who better to learn apologetic strategies from than one who has spent decades in the trenches? This volume comes highly recommended!"

Gary R. Habermas, distinguished research professor and chair, Philosophy Dept., Liberty University & Theological Seminary, and author of *The Case for the Resurrection of Jesus*

"*Forensic Faith* has the kind of unique insight we have come to expect from cold-case detective J. Warner Wallace. Drawing from skills learned from decades of successfully investigating cold-case homicides, Wallace shows exactly how to go about making a compelling case to Christianity's critics. This isn't the 'what,' but the 'how'—the part most Christians are missing. If you want a practical guide to being a more effective Christian case maker, *Forensic Faith* is the book you're looking for."

Melinda Penner, Executive Director of Stand to Reason and STR's senior blogger

"I didn't think J. Warner Wallace could top his masterpiece *Cold-Case Christianity*. I was wrong. In *Forensic Faith*, Wallace gets right to the point. It's not enough for Christians to believe accidentally; they must know their faith evidentially. But there's a problem: Many Christians don't know how to defend the faith. Worse still, many don't want to know. Their ignorance is sustained by denial. Wallace graciously, but firmly, says we must do better. Then he masterfully shows us how. Whether you work at Starbucks, drive a truck, or attend school, we are all apologists now. You may be a prosecutor or a defender, but either way, you have a case to make. There is no finer book for getting started."

Scott Klusendorf, president of Life Training
Institute and author of *The Case for Life*

"Our Summit students love J. Warner Wallace for the same reason criminals hate him. As one of America's most well-known cold-case detectives, his proven tactics have helped bring the guilty to justice even decades after their crimes. Now Wallace shows how those same detective skills can help you confidently share Christianity's truth. *Forensic Faith* is a faith-building page turner."

Jeff Myers, PhD, president of Summit Ministries

"In *Forensic Faith*, J. Warner Wallace continues his relentless pursuit to transform millions of complacent, unprepared Christians into competent advocates for the truth of the gospel. This book is for those who are serious about accepting this challenge and doing the hard work necessary to become informed, inspired, and involved."

Rice Broocks, pastor and founder of Every Nation worldwide
family of churches, and author of *God's Not Dead*

"As a former atheist and a police officer, J. Warner Wallace understands the importance of evidence—whether it's the evidence needed to convict a criminal, or the evidence needed to change the heart of a skeptic. In this important new book, Jim offers an impassioned plea for Christians to get a hold of biblical faith—which isn't blind faith but faith based on evidence: in other words, forensic faith. In the increasingly secular and skeptical age we live in, with many (especially young adults) abandoning the church, it's vital that Christians don't just know what we believe but why we believe it—for there's only one good reason to believe in Christianity, and that's if it's true. *Forensic Faith* is designed to wake up slumbering Christians, encourage them to get to grips with the life of mind and the reasons why we can be sure Christianity is true—and then, with confidence and conviction, engage their friends and colleagues with the gospel. This is a much needed message in many parts of the church—and thus I hope that *Forensic Faith* will help many become passionate Christian case makers."

Andy Bannister, Christian apologist at Ravi Zacharias
Ministries and author of *The Atheist Who Didn't Exist*

"I have been waiting for this book for some time. Wallace practically and succinctly makes the case for why every Christian can be a 'case maker' for Christ. As a pastor, I know many in my congregation who want to share their faith with non-Christians, but they don't simply because they do not feel equipped. This is why every church leader needs *Forensic Faith*. In it, I have found the textbook I have needed for years to help people make the evidential case for the truth of the Christian faith."

Scott Luck, lead pastor of Stones Crossing Church, Greenwood, Indiana

"J. Warner brings renewed energy and duty back to knowing how to give an answer for what we believe. His practical detective approach challenges every disciple of Jesus to no longer be the 'accidental Christian' but to have a clear and compelling answer. This book will be a great tool for any Christ follower who desires to make an evidential case for why they believe. It's a call to action for all of us."

Troy A. Murphy, pastor of Green Bay Community
Church and chaplain for the Green Bay Packers

"There are many excellent apologetics books available today, but most Christians still aren't interested enough in learning to make a case for and defend their faith to read those books—a tragic fact for the church in an increasingly hostile secular world. *Forensic Faith* is the urgently needed book that boldly speaks to the church at large about this dangerous disconnect. In the same captivating style as *Cold-Case Christianity* and *God's Crime Scene*, Det. Wallace makes the ultimate case for apologetics itself and masterfully lays out a practical guide to help every Christian embrace their calling as a case maker. It's compelling, concise, and extremely accessible. *Forensic Faith* is the book I wish I could hand to every Christian today."

Natasha Crain, blogger, speaker, and author
of *Keeping Your Kids on God's Side*

"In *Forensic Faith* award winning cold-case detective and bestselling author J. Warner Wallace makes a compelling case for becoming a Christian case maker. Filled with practical advice and powerful evidence, this innovative approach will help everyday Christians learn why they believe and how to share the reason for their hope with others."

Dr. Jonathan Morrow, director of Creative
Strategies at Impact 360 Institute, popular
speaker, and author of *Welcome to College*

"Christians often say 'You can't argue people into heaven.' While that may be true, it's also true that many people won't come to Christ until they hear some good arguments! J. Warner Wallace was one of those people—and now, in *Forensic Faith*, he shows us how to use effective arguments, logic, and evidence to point our friends to the truth of Christianity. This is powerful information from a world class detective, but it's written for ordinary believers who want to become better case makers for Christ. I highly recommend it."

Mark Mittelberg, bestselling author of *Confident Faith*,
Becoming a Contagious Christian (with Bill Hybels),
and *Today's Moment of Truth* (with Lee Strobel)

"J. Warner Wallace is one of the most engaging writers I've ever read: to read him is like hearing him argue a public case. It is tragic that we have such strong evidence supporting Christian faith and yet many church-attending Christians never learn to articulate such evidence for people who—like me in my atheist days—desperately needed to hear it. More tragic still are young minds swayed by the mere assertions of Christianity's often grossly misinformed, uncritical yet self-assured critics. Wallace's case for making a case offers a desperately needed correction to a church culture too negligent about articulating truth."

Dr. Craig S. Keener, professor of New Testament,
Asbury Theological Seminary, and author of *The IVP
Bible Background Commentary: New Testament*

"J. Warner Wallace has done it again! In a masterful way of blending the past with the present and the evidence with the investigation, *Forensic Faith* gives you not only reasons to believe but tactics to explain it. Unlike many apologetic works, this book weaves in compelling *Dateline* type stories with real detective skills. This is a must read for all Christians!"

Rusty George, lead pastor of Real Life Church
and author of *When You, Then God*

"J. Warner Wallace is the C. S. Lewis of our times. *Forensic Faith* is to this generation what *Mere Christianity* was to its. His blend of apologetics and detective investigation in providing compelling evidence for the Christian faith is exactly what both the world and the church need right now."

Joe Amaral, host of *100 Huntley Street* and author of *Understanding Jesus*

"I have been patiently awaiting the completion of *Forensic Faith*. After J. Warner Wallace's first two books, I was eager to hear more from 'The Cold-Case Detective.' Now I can say, *Forensic Faith* is excellent, as expected, and I wholeheartedly recommend it! Detective Wallace makes a compelling case for making a compelling case for our faith, so that our faith will be more than accidental, but evidential. As our culture becomes more skeptical of our commitment to our faith, the church must become more and more convinced by the evidence for our faith. Every Christian must know, not only what they believe, but why they believe it. And the evidence is compelling! Thanks again, Detective Wallace, for teaching us to think like seasoned investigators in relentless pursuit of, and in confident defense of, truth."

Dr. David W. Fleming, senior pastor of Champion
Forest Baptist Church, Houston, Texas

FORENSIC FAITH

FORENSIC FAITH

A Homicide Detective Makes the Case for a
More Reasonable, Evidential Christian Faith

J. WARNER WALLACE

DAVID C COOK

transforming lives together

FORENSIC FAITH
Published by David C Cook
4050 Lee Vance Drive
Colorado Springs, CO 80918 U.S.A.

David C Cook U.K., Kingsway Communications
Eastbourne, East Sussex BN23 6NT, England

The graphic circle C logo is a registered trademark of David C Cook.

All rights reserved. Except for brief excerpts for review purposes,
no part of this book may be reproduced or used in any form
without written permission from the publisher.

The website addresses recommended throughout this book are offered as a resource to you. These websites are not
intended in any way to be or imply an endorsement on the part of David C Cook, nor do we vouch for their content.

Unless otherwise noted, Scripture quotations are taken from the New American Standard Bible®, copyright
© 1960, 1995 by The Lockman Foundation. Used by permission. (www.Lockman.org.) Scripture quotations
marked ESV are taken from ESV® Bible (The Holy Bible, English Standard Version®), copyright © 2001 by
Crossway, a publishing ministry of Good News Publishers. Used by permission. All rights reserved.
The author has added italics and bold treatment to Scripture quotations for emphasis.

LCCN 2016961914
ISBN 978-1-4347-0988-2
eISBN 978-0-7814-1418-0

© 2017 James Warner Wallace
Published in association with the literary agency of Mark Sweeney & Associates, Bonita Springs, FL 34135.

Illustrations by J. Warner Wallace
The Team: Tim Peterson, Amy Konyndyk, Nick Lee, Jack Campbell, Susan Murdock
Cover Design: Jon Middel
Cover Photo: Getty Images

Printed in the United States of America

First Edition 2017

3 4 5 6 7 8 9 10 11 12

020618

CONTENTS

Go to **www.ForensicFaithBook.com** to download a free facilitator's guide to help coordinate a group study with the *Forensic Faith* curriculum kit and participant's guide. Now available.

FOREWORD

To loosely paraphrase the late Mark Twain, "The news of the demise of apologetics has been greatly exaggerated." For decades now, skeptics who prematurely proclaim their beliefs as "settled science" have been assisted by Christians who prematurely proclaim apologetics—the practice of presenting arguments for the Christian worldview and against non-Christian worldviews—no longer helpful, if it ever was in the first place. They couldn't be more wrong.

It certainly sounds spiritual to say things like, "Arguments never saved anyone," or, "No one is ever argued into the kingdom." Such clichés are, however, silly straw men. I don't know a single apologist who thinks of their arguments as salvific. Perhaps there are one or two who do, but I've never met them. More importantly, however, such statements display a misunderstanding of who we are as people. Certainly, faith involves more than our brains, but it does not involve less.

Humans are not necessarily rational, but they are curious. Humans may not be able to shake off some level of subjectivity in their personal perspectives and experiences, but they consistently share those experiences with others, argue for their legitimacy, and attempt to make sense of them. To be human is to do more than just think like animals do. To be human is to reason, to reflect, and to ask questions about life and its meaning.

Because everyone we meet is one of these question-asking, meaning-seeking creatures, apologetics will always be helpful to those who seek to fulfill Christ's command to make disciples. Unfortunately, too many Christians have bought into the secular myth that religious truth is in the realm of "belief," a realm separate and incompatible with evidence and reason, and therefore unknowable in any true sense. This assumes that while we Christians deal with myth, secularists deal with facts. While our deeply held commitments are mere beliefs, their deeply held commitments are based on reality. That sort of thinking has already given up the best thing Christianity has going for it: that it's true. Actually true. Not true just for those who believe it, not "true for you but not for me." Christianity is really True. With a capital *T*. True for everyone, whether they believe it or not. Christianity describes reality as it actually is.

A few years ago, several ministry friends and colleagues asked if I knew of Jim Wallace. "Of course," I would reply, though I had in mind Jim Wallis, the theologically liberal social activist who founded the Sojourners organization. "Not that one," one of them told me while handing me the book *Cold-Case Christianity*. "This one."

I must admit, when I learned that *this* Jim Wallace was an LA homicide detective now applying the tools of his trade to the field of apologetics, I was concerned. An approach like this, I feared, could easily take an unfortunate turn to the hokey; heavy on cliché and light on depth. Within just a few chapters, however, it was clear to me that my concern was unfounded. Jim knows his stuff. He's worked hard to become one of the most well-respected, studied, and articulate defenders of Christian truth. That's why so many people, Christian and skeptic alike, follow him on social media, read his books and blogs, and flock to hear him speak.

In his first two books, Jim applied his considerable skill in relentlessly pursuing the truth behind horrific crimes to relentlessly pursuing truth about the Gospels and the existence of God. In *Forensic Faith*, he opens up his tool kit and shares those skills with us. Like all the best teachers, Jim wants you to join him in his work. Along with Paul, Jim challenges us to examine everything carefully (1 Thessalonians 5) and to be fully convinced in our own minds (Romans 14:5) about the truth we say we embrace—and then share that conviction with others.

So jump in. Along the way, you will find yourself better at evaluating evidence, thinking through arguments, and making the case for Christian truth. And, I am willing to bet, you may also find yourself better at being you. After all, it was God who gave us these brains in the first place. We should use them.

John Stonestreet
President of the Colson Center for Christian Worldview
Author of *Restoring All Things*

SPECIAL THANKS

I owe a debt of gratitude to Melinda Penner, Rice Broocks, Hank Hanegraaff, Frank Turek, and Mark Mittelberg for their input and effort to improve *Forensic Faith*. I would also like to thank the endorsers for their encouragement and support, and John Stonestreet for his friendship and wisdom. As always, I am humbled to be associated with you in this important mission.

This book is the final installment in a trilogy of books making the case for God's existence (*God's Crime Scene*) and the case for Christianity (*Cold-Case Christianity*). As I wrote these books, I often had a particular group of young people in mind: my own children. Thanks to Jimmy, David, Annie, and Mia for reminding me of the importance of my role as your father. I hope I have served you well.

On those days when God feels far away, or at those times when your doubts seem stronger than His voice, I hope these books will remind you that Christianity is true, in spite of whatever you're going through. If there is one gift I wish to give you, it's the certainty that comes with knowing the truth and developing a forensic faith.

TO PROTECT AND TO SERVE

"Let's go interview the husband."

Alan Jeffries closed the red cold-case notebook and glared at me with obvious impatience. I stared back incredulously. After a long pause, he barked, "What? Why are you giving me that look? Do you have any idea how many of these murders I've worked?"

"Al, we've been working together for years. I know *exactly* how many cases you've investigated. But you just finished reading the notebook, and we haven't even assembled a list of evidences or charted the potential suspects. You've already decided the husband did it." Alan was the most experienced member of our homicide team, but by this point in my career, I had been fairly successful in working the most difficult cases our agency had to offer. I wasn't afraid to challenge the man I came to see as a friend and seasoned colleague.

Alan didn't budge. "Are you ready to go talk to this guy or what?"

To be fair, I could understand where Alan was coming from. The victim in this case was a middle-aged housewife with no known enemies. Most people are killed by someone familiar to them; her husband was a likely suspect on that basis alone. But Alan's certainty about the identity of our killer was entirely premature.

Months later, after an exhaustive investigation of the evidence and every potential suspect, we concluded our victim's husband was, in fact, the man who had killed her. Alan was right all along. We ultimately convicted the husband after a lengthy trial. At the sentencing hearing, Alan leaned over and whispered, "I told you so."

While Alan maintained the husband was our killer from the very beginning, he was only *accidentally* correct in the earliest days of our analysis. By the end, after a long, intense investigation, Alan could boast he was also *evidentially* correct. He had the right suspect all along, but what he once believed *accidentally*, he now knew with *evidential certainty*.

One might argue Alan had good reason to conclude the husband was the killer. Alan's experience and intuition inclined him to target the husband, and Alan was, after all, correct in the end. But his intuition alone wouldn't be enough to convince a jury, and, worse yet, his intuitions had actually failed him (and us) in the past (see chapter 1 of *Cold-Case Christianity*). There's a big difference between *accidental* and *evidential* belief, even though both may lead you to the same conclusion. There are times when accidental belief will land you in the right place, but it seldom stands up to aggressive challenges, and it is often less than persuasive.

Both of Us Can Say It's True, But Only One of Us Will Be Evidentially Confident (and Persuasive) When Challenged

ARE YOU A "CALIFORNIAN CHRISTIAN"?

I actually understand what it's like to be in the right place *accidentally*. As I travel to speaking engagements in cold and remote sections of the country, I'm increasingly grateful to have been born and raised in sunny Southern California. Here, it's 75 degrees and dry nearly every day of the year, and it has some of the nation's best beaches. It's the land of opportunity, with more recreational, educational, and employment opportunities than just about anywhere. I'm happy to identify myself as a Californian.

But if you were to quiz me about the nature of California, you'll quickly find I am not the most *informed* resident in the state. What year was California founded? I don't know. How many counties are in California? I'm not sure. How many people live here? I have no idea. How is a bill passed in our state? How is the state legislature organized? I've never really thought about those things. What's the state bird, the state tree, the state flower, or the state motto? I can't tell you. I guess when it comes right down to it, I'm a pretty terrible Californian. But make no mistake about it; I'm a Californian. It's undeniable. I was born and raised here.

Now think about it for a minute. Are you a Christian the same way I'm a Californian? Were you born and raised in the church yet are still unable to answer the most pressing questions someone might ask about the nature of Christianity? Are you "in the right place" but not really sure *why* it's the right place? Does your affiliation with Christianity feel more like an *accident* than an *informed decision*?

WHY ARE YOU A BELIEVER?

I've been speaking around the country for a number of years now. I often address church groups of one nature or another, and when I do, I usually begin by asking a simple question: "Why are you a Christian?" The response I get is sometimes disappointing. Typically, attendees provide responses in one of the following broad categories:

Answer 1: "I was raised in the church" / "My parents were Christians" / "I've been a Christian as long as I can remember"

Answer 2: "I've had an experience that convinced me" / "The Holy Spirit confirmed it for me" / "God demonstrated His existence to me"

Answer 3: "I was changed by Jesus" / "I used to be [fill in your choice of immoral lifestyle], and God changed my life"

Answer 4: "Because I just *know* the Bible is true" / "Because God called me to believe"

As often as I ask this question, I seldom receive anything other than these four responses. If *you* were asked this question, which answer would *you* give? Some of these are good answers, but others are not. If you're a Christian simply because you've been raised in the church, how can you be sure Christianity is true? If you're a Christian because you've had a transformative experience, how do you know if this experience is truly from the God described on the pages of the New Testament?

As an atheist for most of my life, I learned to be skeptical of people who told me they believed something simply because they grew up a certain way or had an "experience." I wasn't raised in a Christian home, and the man I respected most (my father) was a cynical detective. He was (and still is) also a committed atheist. I grew up as a skeptic and noticed something important along the way: the members of every religion seem to give the *same* answers. The four responses provided by my *Christian* audiences today are also the four answers my *Mormon* friends offer when asked why they believe *Mormonism* is true. In fact, the vast majority of believers in any religion—from Buddhist to Baptist—are likely to offer the same responses. While these kinds of answers are *common*, they are not *sufficient*. Mormonism and Christianity, for example, make entirely contradictory claims related to the nature of Jesus, God the Father, the Holy Spirit, salvation, and a myriad of other important theological truths. Both groups could be *wrong*, or *one* could be correct, but they can't *both* be right, given their contradictory beliefs. Yet both groups offer the same kinds of answers when asked, "Why are you a Christian/ Mormon?"

It seems that *all* believers (regardless of religious affiliation) typically answer this question in the same way, and that's the problem. If our answers sound like the answers given by every other religious group, we need better answers.

You know the one response I seldom, if ever, get when I ask my believing audiences why they are Christians? It's this one: "I am a Christian because it is *true*." Few people seem to have taken the time to investigate the claims of Christianity to determine if they are *evidentially* true. In fact, as I present the case for Christianity around the country, people repeatedly approach me after my presentations to tell me they never knew there was so much evidence supporting what they believe.

These Christian brothers and sisters are similar to my partner, Alan. Their intuitions and experiences incline them to believe Christianity is true long before they've actually investigated the case. Like Alan, they're correct, but when challenged to tell others why they believe Christianity is true, they sound like every other non-Christian theistic believer. Their defenses seldom stand up to aggressive challenges and are often less than persuasive. Why should atheists accept the testimonial experiences of Christians when Christians themselves don't accept the testimonial experiences of other believing groups—or of atheists?

IT'S TIME TO PUT UP OR SHUT UP

Now, more than ever, Christians must shift from *accidental belief* to *evidential trust*. It's time to know *why* you believe *what* you believe. Christians must embrace a *forensic faith*. In case you haven't been paying attention, Christians living in America and Europe are facing a growingly skeptical culture. Polls and surveys continue to confirm the decline of Christianity.[1] When believers explain why they think Christianity is true, unbelievers are understandably wary of the reasons they've been given so far.

As Christians, we'd better embrace a more thoughtful version of Christianity, one that understands the value of evidence, the importance of philosophy, and the virtue of good reasoning. The brilliant thinker and writer C. S. Lewis was prophetic when he called for a more intellectual church in 1939. On the eve of World War II, Lewis drew a parallel between the challenges facing Christianity in his own day and the challenges facing his country as war approached:

> If all the world were Christian it might not matter if all the world were uneducated. But, as it is, a cultural life will exist outside the Church whether it exists inside or not. To be ignorant and simple now—not to be able to meet the enemies on their own ground—would be to throw down our weapons, and to betray our uneducated brethren who have, under God, no defence but us against the intellectual attacks of the heathen. Good philosophy must exist, if for no other reason, because bad philosophy needs to be answered. The cool intellect must work not only against the cool intellect on the other side, but against the muddy heathen mysticisms which deny intellect altogether.[2]

Over seventy years ago, Lewis recognized two challenges facing the church: (1) Christians are largely unprepared to make the case for what they believe; and (2) many in the church still deny the need to be prepared in the first place. We are a largely anti-intellectual group, even though the history of Christianity is replete with some of the greatest thinkers who ever lived. In spite of our rich intellectual history, we have arrived at a point where there is a need to make a case for *making a case*.

I'm not the only one to notice how anti-intellectual the church is today. Atheist activist and philosophy professor Peter Boghossian wrote a book in 2013 entitled *A Manual for Creating Atheists*. It was published around the same time my first book, *Cold-Case Christianity*, hit the bookshelves. Boghossian describes his book as "the first-ever guide not for talking people into faith—but for talking them out of it." He hopes to teach atheists "to engage the faithful in conversations that will help them value reason and rationality, cast doubt on their religious beliefs, mistrust their faith, abandon superstition and irrationality, and ultimately embrace reason." In a YouTube video promoting the approach, Boghossian made an interesting observation: Christians fail to process truth claims rationally; instead of assessing the evidence and drawing the most reasonable inference, they typically rely on personal experience, emotional response, and "blind faith." For this reason, he encourages atheists to engage Christians not on the evidence but on the *way* Christians evaluate truth claims in the first place.

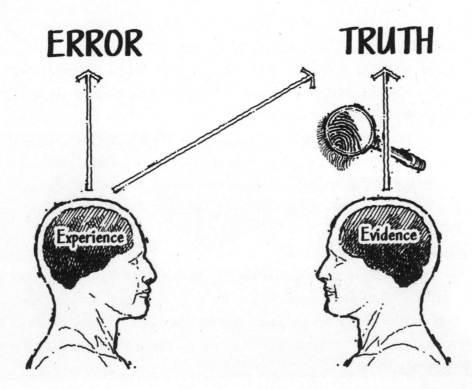

Sadly, my own experience in the church confirms what Boghossian has described. Boghossian, and others like him, believe they need only show Christians how to examine evidence and the rest will take care of itself. Confident of the evidence supporting *their* view, they can't imagine Christianity will survive a forensic investigation in the "age of reason." But as someone who has examined the evidence of God's existence and the reliability of the New Testament documents as a detective, I hold a similar, although opposite, view. If Christians will simply learn how to approach their beliefs evidentially and take the same forensic approach detectives take when examining an event from the past, the rest will take care of itself. I'm confident the claims of Christianity are supported by the evidence, and I believe a *forensic faith* will comfortably survive in the age of reason. Boghossian and I are engaged in a race of sorts. Both of us understand the importance of the evidence, and we are trying to reach the same group of accidental Christians. The only question is who will reach them first.

THE CASE FOR CASE MAKING

I want to share an awkward truth with you. Although this is little more than anecdotal evidence, I do think it illustrates what C. S. Lewis described all those years ago. About half of my speaking engagements are in churches where I am asked to talk to the congregation about the reliability of the Gospels, the reasonable inference of the resurrection, or the evidence for God's existence. In many of these churches, the people I meet aren't really interested in Christian "apologetics" (the discipline of making the case for Christianity). In fact, most are still completely unfamiliar with the word, and some even reject the value of such an effort. On more than one occasion, I've heard a well-meaning believer say something akin to, "Well, that's nice, but I don't really need any evidence. I just believe Christianity is true. I don't really think you can argue someone into the kingdom anyway." When I encounter this kind of response, I know I have my work cut out for me. Before I can make the case for Christianity, I have to make the case for *making the case*.

That's what I hope to do here in *Forensic Faith*. In my previous books, I made the case for Christianity (*Cold-Case Christianity*) and God's existence (*God's Crime Scene*). But if you're not convinced of the need for a more intellectually robust, thoughtful version of Christianity, my prior case-making books will be of little value to you.

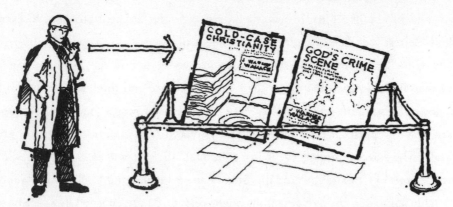

If You Understand the Importance of Evidence, You're Far More Likely to Examine the Case

When Christians see a crisis, we typically respond passionately. We readily rescue those devastated by natural disaster, feed the hungry, and do our best to meet the needs of the impoverished. We have a history of doing whatever it takes to respond to real human challenges. Well, there's another real challenge on the horizon. Christians (especially *young* Christians) are leaving the church in record numbers. Surveys and polls have been exposing this disturbing trend for many years now:

> Most teenagers are incredibly inarticulate about their religious beliefs and practices. They typically cannot defend what they believe.
>
> Young, uninformed believers also reject important Christian claims. Sixty-three percent of teenage Christians don't believe Jesus is the Son of God; 51 percent don't believe Jesus rose from the dead; 68 percent don't believe the Holy Spirit is a real Being.
>
> Between 60 percent and 80 percent of people aged 15 to 30 will leave the church for at least a season, and most will never return.
>
> Only 33 percent of young, churched Christians said the church will play a part in their lives when they leave home.

If current trends related to the belief systems and practices of young people continue, church attendance will decline by 50 percent in the next decade. College professors are nearly five times more likely to be professing atheists or agnostics than people in the general population. The vast majority of university professors reject the Bible as "the actual word of God."

When surveyed, the largest segment of young, ex-Christian respondents said they left Christianity because they had intellectual doubt, skepticism, and unanswered questions.[3]

If you're a Christian, you already know the sad truth. Someone in your family (a son, daughter, grandson, granddaughter, niece, or nephew) has already walked away, in spite of all the years you spent raising them in the church. I believe we can change this alarming trajectory, but we have to be willing to address the problem head on. If we are willing to do what it takes to respond to the trials facing the poor, the hungry, and the homeless, why won't we do what it takes to respond to the challenges facing our own Christian family?

I write about the evidence for Christianity several times a week and post these articles (along with videos and podcasts) on my website (www.ColdCaseChristianity.com). I often get emails from readers. One young man named Andrew Deane recently sent this message:[4]

My Dad was a Southern Baptist Preacher and while I was growing up I basically lived at the church. I knew all of the bible stories and was even baptized when I was eight … After graduating high school, I went to college to get a degree in mechanical engineering. One might think a degree of this kind would involve little to no discussion of whether or not God exists, or if Jesus was a real person, but I encountered these and many more objections.

I had a literature class where the professor gave a presentation on how Jesus was copied from other gods and how this explained away the "mythology" of Jesus. I had an electromagnetics course in which the professor viciously attacked the concept of intelligent design … I had a space technology class in which the professor vehemently argued for the existence of aliens but refused to acknowledge the existence of God. These are just a few examples from the many interactions I had with my professors.

Unfortunately, most of our fellow brothers and sisters in Christ are severely lacking in training, and when they encounter even the weakest arguments, they are not prepared … As a Christian in the college setting, you are being constantly challenged, constantly poked and prodded. It is easy to throw your hands in the air, becoming convinced your faith is a lie when you are being trampled every day by both professors and by peers. All Christians, but especially ones in college, must know what they believe and why they believe it if they have any hope of surviving with their faith intact … I think of college almost like an atheist ambush. The Christians are walking in totally unaware of the danger until it is too late and the damage has already been done.

That's why I wanted to take the time to thank you … When I entered college, I was struggling with many of the objections I encountered. I discovered your podcast and your careful research. The evidentiary approach was incredibly helpful. As a result, I actually exited college with my faith even stronger than when I began. I want to encourage you to keep up the good work.

Young Christians struggle when challenged (as Andrew did), but this doesn't have to be the case. If properly equipped, they could actually *grow* in their faith and confidence, even in the midst of strong opposition. You and I have the opportunity to reach the young people we love, including young Christians like Andrew, if we are willing to embrace the mission.

Our children, and our brothers and sisters in Christ, are in the right place; they believe something *true*. If they've come to understand their own need for a Savior and have repented and placed their trust in Jesus alone for their salvation, they are saved for eternity. But if they haven't taken the time to study *why* Christianity is true, like Alan (my partner in the crime scene), they will be ill-equipped to answer objections and less than persuasive with a group that requires far more evidence than ever before. We have to change the course of the church in order to meet this challenge, and the church is much more like an ocean liner than a jet ski. We cannot turn it on a dime. Instead, we must make small course corrections—one degree here and one degree there. *Forensic Faith* is my effort to come alongside the church as a tugboat and shift the direction of our ocean liner one degree at a time.

TO PROTECT AND TO SERVE

In 1955, the Los Angeles Police Department ran a contest for a motto they could use at their police academy. They told contestants the motto should express, in just a few words, the "ideals to which the Los Angeles police service is dedicated." The winning entry was submitted by Officer Joseph Dorobek. "To Protect and to Serve" has been emblazoned on Los Angeles Police cars ever since and has, in many ways, become the adopted motto of law enforcement personnel across the country.

Police officers are called to *serve* and to *protect*. You don't enter this profession unless this mission is part of your DNA. Officers understand their sworn duty, train rigorously in preparation for their mission, and learn how to investigate and discern the truth so they can ultimately communicate this truth to a jury. Every day is a *call to action*.

As a church, we can learn something from this resolute approach to mission. As Christians, we have a similar duty. The apostle Peter said we are called to *serve* one another with "sympathy, brotherly love, a tender heart, and a humble mind" (1 Peter 3:8 ESV) and called to *protect* the truth by "being prepared to make a defense to anyone who asks you for a reason for the hope that is in you" (verse 15 ESV). Christians are called to *serve* and *protect*. If we want to fulfill this duty, we'll need to train rigorously so we can investigate and communicate the truth. I hope *Forensic Faith* is *your* call to action. It's time to change course. It's time to raise the bar. It's time to get serious. It's time to embrace our distinct duty as Christians.

Chapter One
DISTINCTIVE DUTY
*5 Evidential Examples to Help You Embrace
Your Calling as a Christian Case Maker*

"Action springs not from thought, but from a readiness for responsibility."[1]
Dietrich Bonhoeffer

"The soldier is summoned to a life of active duty and so is the Christian."[2]
William Gurnall

"I do solemnly swear that I will support and defend the Constitution of the United States and the Constitution of the State of California against all enemies, foreign and domestic; that I will bear true faith and allegiance to the Constitution of the United States and the Constitution of the State of California; that I take this obligation freely, without any mental reservation or purpose of evasion; and that I will well and faithfully discharge the duties upon which I am about to enter."

Nearly one hundred newly sworn police officers and sheriff's deputies lowered their right hands and took a seat in the front rows of the large civic assembly hall. Our parents and friends were sitting in the upper balcony, proudly watching the graduation ceremony. I was incredibly nervous—not because I just pledged my life to this altruistic cause, but because I was worried about what I might say if called to the stage.

Sure enough, I was about to make an impromptu speech. After a brief description of the award he was about to bestow, the sheriff looked in my direction and said, "The honor recruit of Class 245 is Officer James Warner Wallace."

As recruits, none of us knew in advance who would receive this award. I took a second to catch my breath, then I walked onto the stage and did my best to say something profound. I didn't realize

31

until that very moment just how important the achievement was to me. I was the second Jim Wallace to serve at our agency, continuing a tradition that began in 1961 when my father started his career.

Forensic Faith Profile:

C. S. LEWIS

C. S. Lewis graduated from Oxford University where he majored in literature and classic philosophy. As an atheist, he joined an informal group of writers and intellectuals known as the Inklings. He came to faith, in part, based on his conversations with other great thinkers in this group and shortly thereafter became a passionate Christian case maker. While he wrote many well-known fictional books (e.g., The Chronicles of Narnia series), he is perhaps best known for his case-making classic *Mere Christianity*. Once Lewis decided Christianity was true, he was "all in." His fictional and nonfictional books reflected his passionate Christian worldview.

Is your Christian worldview reflected in everything you do? Make a list of your activities this week. What needs to change in order for you to embrace your duty as a Christian case maker and reflect your passion as a Christian?

I had been a police explorer as a teenager, and when I graduated from the explorer academy, I also received a version of this award. I saw the pride in my father's eyes then, and I wanted to see it again. The third Jim Wallace to serve at our department was also in the auditorium, cradled as a newborn in the arms of my wife, Susie. It would be another twenty-four years before my son, Jimmy, would join our ranks, but on this day, I was glad both Jims were in the audience for the Honor Recruit presentation. I had no idea, however, the challenges this award would cause.

In the first five years of my career, I was challenged at every turn. I was "Wallace's college kid" and an honor recruit, to boot. My peers wanted to test how much I knew about life on the streets. Was I too soft? Could I handle a tough situation? Would I recognize a crime when I saw it? How thoroughly did I know the law? Could I put together a case? The bar was high for me, and at times I feared I would fall short of everyone's expectations. I had a choice: accept the challenge and rise to meet it, or simply shrink back into irrelevance and obscurity. I chose to accept my public duty as a police officer and my personal calling as a member of the Wallace family. To be successful in this environment, I needed to learn what was essential to the profession of law enforcement and what was required of my professional peers. I discovered something very early in my journey: the demands of a law enforcement career would require me to be "all in" or "all out." I needed to decide law enforcement was either *critically* important to me or *unimportant* to me. I knew I would never succeed if I took a halfhearted approach.

If you're a member of the Christian family, you face a similar challenge. The bar is high, and the culture is suspicious of both your family affiliation and your status as a believer. You are a son or daughter of the *King*, and you've been awarded the gift of eternal life. The culture is eager to test you. Are you too soft? Can you handle a tough situation? How thoroughly do you know what you believe? Can you put together a case? If you're going to be successful in this increasingly hostile environment, you're going to have to learn what is essential to Christianity and what is required by our culture. You have a choice: accept the challenge and rise to meet it, or simply shrink back into irrelevance and obscurity. In a culture that is increasingly suspicious of Christianity and increasingly *evidential*, we as believers need to be ready to accept our public duty as ambassadors of Jesus Christ as we accept our personal calling as members of the Christian family. We either need to decide our Christian affiliation is *unimportant* to us or *critically* important to us. We'll never succeed if we take a halfhearted approach. C. S. Lewis put it this way:

> Christianity is a statement which, if false, is of no importance, and, if true, is of infinite importance. The one thing it cannot be is moderately important.[3]

WITH ALL YOUR *MIND*

I was a police officer long before I was a Christian. When I recited the law enforcement oath, I believed it was one of the most important covenants I would ever make. And after sixteen weeks of preparation at the academy, I understood the nature of my duty. Years later when I became a follower of Jesus Christ, I realized I had an even *more* important duty as His ambassador. Jesus summarized our calling as Christians when He described the greatest commandment in Scripture. He put it succinctly:

> "You shall love the Lord your God with all your heart, and with all your soul,

Forensic Faith Definition:
DUTY

Duty has two common meanings. First, it describes the obligatory force of something morally or legally *required*. In this sense, duties compel us to act and do what's *right*. Duty also, however, describes the actions or tasks essential to a person's position or occupation. Police officers, for example, must perform certain *duties* as part of their job.

What are the moral obligations we must embrace as Christians? What has God called us to *be* and what has He called us to *do*? What duties do you perform on a daily basis that reflect your identity as a Christian?

and with all your mind." This is the great and foremost commandment. The second is like it, "You shall love your neighbor as yourself. On these two commandments depend the whole Law and the Prophets."[4]

Interestingly, when Jesus was asked about the greatest commandment, He altered the Old Testament reference found in Deuteronomy:

You shall love the LORD your God with all your heart and with all your soul and with all your might.[5]

All the gospel authors agree that Jesus used the word "mind" in His summary of this Old Testament verse (instead of the word "strength"). The Greek word used by these authors is *dianoia* (διάνοια): a word used to describe our "minds," our "understanding," or our "intelligence." Here in Matthew's gospel, the word is used to describe the "place where thinking occurs."[6] Jesus's intentional word exchange raises the bar for us as Christians. We are not only to love God with all our heart, soul, and *might*, but we are also commanded to use our *mind* and our *intelligence* to *understand* the truth of Christianity. This effort is an act of *worship*. Most of us, as Christians, know what it is to love God with our hearts and soul, but what does it mean to love God with our minds?

Ways to Love God

THE CHRISTIAN *DIFFERENCE* IS THE FOUNDATION OF OUR CHRISTIAN *DUTY*

Christianity is distinct in the nature of its claims and the value it places on reason, intelligence, and evidence. Some religious systems are based purely on the doctrinal, proverbial statements of their founders. The wisdom statements of Buddha, for example, lay the foundation for Buddhism. Hinduism is based on the revelations of the ancient sages as revealed in the *Vedas* and the *Upanishads*. Confucianism is established from the wisdom statements of Confucius. In all these examples, the statements of these religious leaders exist independently of any event in history. In other words, these systems rise or fall on the basis of *ideas* and *concepts* rather than on claims about a particular *historical event*.

Although Christianity makes its own ideological and philosophical claims, these proposals are intrinsically connected to a singular validating event: the resurrection of Jesus Christ.

Why should anyone believe what Jesus said rather than what Buddha, the Hindu sages, or Confucius said? The authority of Jesus is grounded in more than the strength of an *idea*; it's established by the verifiability of an *event*. When Jesus rose from the dead, He established His authority as God, and His resurrection provides us with an important Christian distinctive. The resurrection can be examined for its reliability, and the evidential verifiability of Christianity separates it from every other religious system.

Let me offer an analogy to make the point clearer.

If I told you I had a private vision from God yesterday in which He revealed a number of important truths He wanted me to share with you, how could you ever verify (or falsify) my claim? Personal visions and pietistic

> Forensic Faith Definition:
> **TESTIMONY**
>
> Testimony is described as a statement or declaration of a witness (usually under oath). Eyewitness testimonies are typically used to support a fact or claim. The apostles, for example, testified about the evidence related to the resurrection when making a case for Christianity. As Christians, we typically think of our testimony in terms of our own personal experience of God. While that's good, our testimony could also include our assessment of evidence beyond our personal experience.
>
> If you were required to testify and make a case for the truth of Christianity, what could you offer beyond your own *subjective* personal experience? What kind of *objective* evidence could you present to make the case for the reliability of the Bible or the existence of God?

wisdom statements are difficult to validate evidentially. You have to accept my story or reject it, but in either case, you'll have to do so without the ability to investigate my claims evidentially. You can't, after all, get into my head to see if I am lying about this very personal "revelation." What if, on the other hand, I told you I had been visited by God *physically*? God came to me in the form of a man and, in the presence of my friends, had lunch with me in my backyard. While He was here, He helped me dig a trench for my irrigation line and even put some finishing touches on a treehouse for my kids. Can you see how this kind of *public* claim is categorically different from *private* claims about visions and divine wisdom? The public claims are about historical events that occurred (or didn't occur) in my backyard *in front of witnesses*. As such, they can be investigated forensically and historically. My friends could be interviewed. The irrigation trench could be examined for attributes of "Divine Digging." The treehouse could be examined for evidence of a "Heavenly Helper." My claim about a divine *public* visitation could be examined evidentially and verified in a way *private* revelatory claims cannot.

The Christian's claims are public claims. Christianity is established on the basis of an event in history. We can investigate this event like other historical occurrences (including cold-case murders, my particular area of expertise). This kind of verifiability is a Judeo-Christian distinctive.

The Claims of Most Religions Are Private   The Claims of Christianity Are Public

You may be asking yourself, "Hey, wait a minute. Christianity isn't the only theistic system based on a historical event. What about religions like Mormonism?" While Mormonism, for example, is also based on a historical claim about the past (in this case, an assertion about the early history of the North American continent), these claims are demonstrably *false*. In fact, the same process I used as a skeptic to test the reliability of the Gospels (as described in *Cold-Case Christianity*) I also used to test the reliability of the Book of Mormon. The evidence *verified* Christianity and *falsified* Mormonism. The distinctive attribute of Christianity is not simply that it is *verifiable* but that it *passes* our verification tests. Christianity is both verifiable and *verified*. It is true.

If thoughtful, evidential verifiability is a Christian distinctive, shouldn't a thoughtful, evidential approach to the evidence for Christianity be our distinctive Christian duty? Shouldn't this duty call us to live differently than the adherents of other religious systems? Shouldn't we, as Christians, be the one group who knows *why* our beliefs are true and is most willing to defend *what* we believe? Why, then, are we often uninterested in the evidence? Why do we sound like every other religious group when asked to give a reason for our beliefs? It's time for the distinctly evidential nature of Christianity to result in a distinctly intelligent, reasonable, and evidential family of believers. This Christian *difference* ought to form our Christian *duty*. We are called to embrace a *forensic faith* and to love God with our minds.

Forensic Faith Definition:
EVIDENCE

As a detective I've learned that anything that shows a claim to be true can be offered as evidence. When investigating a particular suspect, I consider eyewitness statements, behaviors observed on the part of the suspect, material evidence at the scene (including biological and physical evidence), and statements made (or omitted) by the person I'm investigating. Just about *everything* has the potential to be an important piece of evidence.

If someone asked you to make a case for the reliability of the New Testament, what kind of evidence would you consider? Can you articulate the archaeological evidence? Can you describe the internal textual evidence from the Gospels? Are you familiar with early non-Christian sources related to the life and ministry of Jesus? (For more information about these evidences, refer to *Cold-Case Christianity*.)

INCONSISTENT EVIDENTIALISTS

I was working in an undercover position when I first began to investigate the Gospels as eyewitness accounts. My wife, Susie, asked me to go to church with her, and I was willing to go, even though most of the Christians I knew didn't seem all that thoughtful. A few of my coworkers were outspoken Christians, and two of them had talked to me on occasion about how much Jesus meant to them. I was an obnoxious and obstinate atheist at the time, and I pushed back with a variety of direct questions designed to test what they believed. I continually asked them for evidence to support their claims: "Why do you think the Bible is true?" "Why do you guys believe Jesus actually rose from the dead?" "Why doesn't an all-powerful God stop all the evil we have to deal with every day as police officers?"

Their answers weren't very good. In fact, I was astonished to find they held a relatively unexamined faith. These seasoned investigators would never claim someone was a suspect in a crime without good evidence, yet they claimed Jesus was *God* on the basis of little more than subjective, personal experience. They seemed to be walking contradictions—inconsistent in their evidential approach to the truth claims of the Bible, even though they, of all people, should have understood the role evidence plays in determining what (if anything) is true.

If that's what Christianity was all about, I wanted nothing to do with it.

But as I read the New Testament for the first time, I was pleasantly surprised. Christian belief was never intended to be "blind," even if some of my Christian friends seemed to be unaware of the evidence supporting their beliefs. In fact, Christianity encourages rational exploration and reasonable examination. Believers are encouraged repeatedly to examine what they believe carefully so they can be fully convinced their beliefs are true. Take a look at the following admonitions in the New Testament:

> **1 Thessalonians 5:19–21**
>
> Do not quench the Spirit; do not despise prophetic utterances. But *examine everything* carefully; hold fast to that which is good.

> **1 John 4:1**
>
> Beloved, do not believe every spirit, but *test the spirits* to see whether they are from God, because many false prophets have gone out into the world.

Romans 14:5

Each person must be *fully convinced in his own mind*.

2 Timothy 3:14

You, however, continue in the things you have learned *and become convinced of*, knowing from whom you have learned them.

Christianity is reasonable, and it's our Christian duty to examine and test what we believe so we can be fully convinced. As a detective, it was often my duty to test the statements of the suspects I arrested. Some of these suspects provided me with alibis in efforts to fool me. But none of them really wanted me to investigate their alibis deeply. None *invited* me to do so. Why? Because they knew they were lying; they were hoping I *wouldn't* follow up on their claims. But that's not the approach of the gospel authors. Unlike my dishonest suspects, the writers of Scripture encourage us to reason through the evidence in order to investigate their claims. Listen to what Jude, the brother of Jesus, said about the value of *reason*:

Jude 4, 10

For certain persons have crept in unnoticed, those who were long beforehand marked out for this condemnation, ungodly persons who turn the grace of our God into licentiousness and deny our only Master and Lord, Jesus Christ … But these men revile the things which they do not understand; and the things which they know by instinct, *like unreasoning animals*, by these things they are destroyed.

Jude uses this word for "unreasoning" in a pejorative manner; to be unreasoning is to act like a brute animal. God clearly wants more from beings created in His image. When I first read these words, I wondered if my Christian coworkers were familiar with them. As professional *investigators*, they were committed evidentialists, but as *Christians*, they seemed to be unaware of the teaching of their own Scripture.

Non-Evidential Belief
in Christianity

Evidential Belief
in a Particular Suspect

The Bible calls us to be *reasonable*. The biblical authors *confidently* challenged us to investigate their claims. The writers of Scripture had nothing to hide. As a result, Christians are encouraged to be reasonable, evidential investigators.

I grew up in a family that emphasized the importance of using evidence to make a case for what we believe. I was born while my father, James David Wallace Sr., was attending police academy. He raised me to understand the value of reason and evidence. You might say it's a part of my family tradition. My son, James David Wallace Jr., was born while I was attending the *same* police academy. Case making is also part of *his* tradition. We've passed this investigative, evidential practice from officer to officer through three generations. Each *younger* Jim Wallace learned from the example offered by an *older* Jim Wallace. We understand our role as members of this law enforcement family, and we embrace our evidential, case-making duty as an important part of our *identity*.

As a member of the Christian family, I also recognize the importance of reason and evidence. It's part of our *Christian* tradition. I've learned from the examples offered by older Christian role models. I understand my place as a member of this Christian family, and I embrace my evidential, case-making duty as an important part of my *Christian* identity. The history of Christianity is filled with examples of people who embraced a *forensic faith* and modeled what it means to be a Christian case maker.

FORENSIC FAITH EVIDENTIAL EXAMPLE #1
CHRIST, THE CASE MAKER

All evidence can be divided into two broad categories: *direct* and *indirect*. Direct evidence is simply the testimony of eyewitnesses. Indirect evidence (also called "circumstantial evidence") is everything else. The Jesus I encountered on the pages of the New Testament was a committed case maker, and He understood these two important categories. He didn't expect His followers to believe what He said (direct evidence) without good reason (the support of indirect evidence). Jesus continually supported His testimony with the indirect evidence of the miracles He performed. He then made the case for the authority of His testimony from the corroborative evidence of these miracles:

John 5:36
But the *testimony* which I have is greater than the *testimony* of John; for the *works* which the Father has given Me to accomplish—*the very works that I do*—*testify* about Me, that the Father has sent Me.

John 10:25
Jesus answered them, "I told you, and you do not believe; the *works* that I do in My Father's name, these *testify* of Me."

John 10:37–38
If I do not do the *works of My Father*, do not believe Me; but if I do them, though you do not believe Me, believe the works, so that you may know and understand that the Father is in Me, and I in the Father.

John 14:11
Believe Me that I am in the Father and the Father is in Me; otherwise *believe because of the works themselves.*

Jesus knew His followers needed more than His direct testimony. He offered the evidence of the miracles to corroborate His claims so His hearers would be fully convinced. In fact, Jesus was so committed to this evidential approach that He stayed with the disciples for over a month following His resurrection to give them additional evidence:

Acts 1:2–3

… until the day when He was taken up to heaven, after He had by the Holy Spirit given orders to the apostles whom He had chosen. To these He also presented Himself alive after His suffering, by many convincing proofs, appearing to them over a period of forty days and speaking of the things concerning the kingdom of God.

Think about that for a minute. Jesus had already demonstrated His deity by *rising from the grave*. I think that would be enough for me. But it wasn't for Jesus. He stayed an additional forty days to give many more "convincing proofs." That's an exceptional commitment to case making.

I was even more impressed with Jesus's commitment to evidence, however, when I discovered how Jesus responded to *doubt*. As a cold-case detective, I've learned to evaluate words carefully when considering the statements made by victims, witnesses, and suspects. What someone *didn't* say is often more important than what they *did* say. In fact, I often stop and ask myself, "What were some of the options available when this person made their statement? What could they have said in this particular circumstance and what does their choice of words tell us about their thoughts or the truth of the situation?" As an investigator of the New Testament, I found myself asking the same kinds of questions as I studied Jesus's response to doubt.

There are two important accounts in the Gospels that describe people close to Jesus who, in spite of everything they had seen, still had nagging doubts about Jesus's identity and claims to deity. The first involved Jesus's cousin, John the Baptist. Jesus was incredibly fond of John and once said, "Among those born of women there has not arisen anyone greater than John the Baptist" (Matthew 11:11). John was a godly man raised in a godly home. His mother, Elizabeth, knew that Jesus was "Lord" while Jesus was still in His mother Mary's womb (Luke 1:39–45). Surely John grew up with this information, and Jesus's status as Messiah was confirmed to him when he saw God's Spirit descend on Jesus at Jesus's baptism (Luke 3:22). If anyone should have been sure of Jesus's identity, it would have been John the Baptist.

But when John was arrested by Herod, he sent two of his own disciples to ask Jesus a question. In spite of everything he knew about Jesus, John's query revealed his doubt: "Are You the Expected One, or do we look for someone else?" John, of all people, should have already known the answer. But there he was, asking Jesus to calm his doubt.

When I first read this passage as a detective, I thought about all the things Jesus *could have* done or said in response to John's expression of doubt. He could have condemned John, but He didn't. He could have scolded him for his failure to trust what John's own mother seemed to know so clearly. Jesus didn't do that either. Finally, Jesus could have instructed John to simply trust in what he had been taught as a child, or in what he had "experienced" from God in the past. But that's not how Jesus responded.

Instead, Jesus provided John's disciples with *evidence*:

> At that very time He cured many people of diseases and afflictions and evil spirits; and He gave sight to many who were blind. And He answered and said to them, "Go and report to John what you have seen and heard: the blind receive sight, the lame walk, the lepers are cleansed, and the deaf hear, the dead are raised up, the poor have the gospel preached to them. Blessed is he who does not take offense at Me."[7]

Jesus performed miracles as a demonstration of His identity (these miracles were consistent with the messianic expectations found in Isaiah 29:18 and Isaiah 35:5–6). When asked, in essence, "How can we know this is true?" Jesus responded by making a case with *evidence*.

John the Baptist was not the only person to express his doubt. The apostle Thomas (also known as Didymus) is famous for his own episode of uncertainty. Thomas was one of Jesus's closest associates and an important member of Jesus's hand-picked team of twelve. But Thomas had a hard time believing Jesus could actually raise Himself from the grave, and he didn't believe the other apostles when they reported seeing Jesus alive after the crucifixion. His doubt was reported in John's gospel:

> But Thomas, one of the twelve, called Didymus, was not with them when Jesus came. So the other disciples were saying to him, "We have seen the Lord!" But he said to them, "Unless I see in His hands the imprint of the nails, and put my finger into the place of the nails, and put my hand into His side, I will not believe."[8]

Jesus's response to Thomas's doubt is similar to His response to John the Baptist. He didn't expect Thomas simply to trust what he had been told by others or to lean on his own private experiences. Instead, Jesus once again provided a public, evidential demonstration:

Forensic Faith Profile:
JESUS OF NAZARETH

Jesus provided us with an example of how we ought to live as His disciples. We typically think of Jesus as a role model when it comes to our love of others, our devotion to the Father, or our commitment to moral purity. But how often do we think of Jesus as a role model for how we ought to *think* or *make a case for truth*?

Given what you've learned about Jesus in this chapter, how might you follow His example as a Christian case maker? How would Jesus's example change the way you help others work through their doubt? How would His example change the way you defend His deity?

> After eight days His disciples were again inside, and Thomas with them. Jesus came, the doors having been shut, and stood in their midst and said, "Peace be with you." Then He said to Thomas, "Reach here with your finger, and see My hands; and reach here your hand and put it into My side; and do not be unbelieving, but believing." Thomas answered and said to Him, "My Lord and my God!"[9]

Thomas, when confronted with the evidence, surrendered his doubt. Now to be fair, the story doesn't end there, and the next line of Scripture is sometimes cited by people who argue against the kind of evidential approach to Christianity I have described so far. Immediately following Thomas's confession of faith, Jesus said the following:

Jesus said to him, "Because you have seen Me, have you believed? Blessed are they who did not see, and yet believed."[10]

At first glance, it almost appears as though Jesus is saying something equivalent to, "Hey, you may have needed some evidence, Thomas, but those who believe *without* evidence are even *more* blessed than you!" This isn't what Jesus means, however, and the next verse makes this clear:

Therefore many other signs Jesus also performed in the presence of the disciples, which are not written in this book; but these have been written so that you may believe that Jesus is the Christ, the Son of God; and that believing you may have life in His name.[11]

In one breath, Jesus said, "Blessed are those who did not see and yet believed," and in the very next passage, Jesus "therefore" continued to make the case with the "many other signs" He performed in the presence of the disciples. Why would Jesus continue to provide additional evidence after saying those who believe *without* evidence are blessed? The answer is found, once again, in the gospel of John. In Jesus's famous prayer to the Father in chapter 17, Jesus prayed for unity and He carefully included those of us who would become Christians long after He ascended into heaven:

I do not ask on behalf of these [the first disciples] alone, but for those also who believe in Me through their word; that they may all be one; even as You, Father, are in Me and I in You, that they also may be in Us, so that the world may believe that You sent Me. (John 17:20–21)

In this prayer, Jesus was talking about all the people (like you and me) who believe in Jesus not because of the evidence we saw with our *own* eyes but because of the testimony (direct evidence) offered by the disciples ("their word"). Yes, Thomas was blessed to believe based on what he saw, but we are also blessed because we believe based on what he (and the authors of the Gospels) reported as eyewitnesses. That's why Jesus continued to perform "many other signs" in front of His disciples. He wanted them to have a lot to talk about. Jesus is our example. He repeatedly used evidence to make His case, even when His point was simply to encourage someone in a time of doubt.

Christ
the Case Maker

The Rich, Evidential History of Christian Case-Making

FORENSIC FAITH EVIDENTIAL EXAMPLE #2:
THE COMMISSIONED CASE MAKERS

Jesus's commitment to case making wasn't lost on His followers. In fact, the disciples carried Jesus's message into a hostile world, fully aware of their evidential role as eyewitnesses. The gospel accounts were written as *historical* narratives. The life of Jesus was chronicled alongside other historical events that located Jesus geographically and historically. Along the way, key eyewitnesses were identified:

John 1:6–7
There came a man sent from God, whose name was John. He came as a *witness*, to *testify* about the Light, so that all might believe through him.

Throughout the first century, other eyewitnesses provided direct evidence of Jesus's life, ministry, and (eventually) resurrection. These people were commissioned by Jesus Himself to grow the kingdom on the basis of their eyewitness observations:

Luke 24:44–49

Now He said to them, "These are My words which I spoke to you while I was still with you, that all things which are written about Me in the Law of Moses and the Prophets and the Psalms must be fulfilled." Then He opened their minds to understand the Scriptures, and He said to them, "Thus it is written, that the Christ would suffer and rise again from the dead the third day, and that repentance for forgiveness of sins would be proclaimed in His name to all the nations, beginning from Jerusalem. You are *witnesses* of these things. And behold, I am sending forth the promise of My Father upon you; but you are to stay in the city until you are clothed with power from on high."

Forensic Faith Profile:
SIMON PETER

Simon Peter should give all of us, as imperfect followers of Jesus, great hope and encouragement. Although Peter witnessed the miracles of Jesus firsthand, he apparently learned slowly, making mistake after mistake and even denying he knew Jesus when questioned on the night before the crucifixion. But after seeing Jesus raised from the dead, Peter was transformed. The resurrection was an evidential turning point for the disciples, but especially for Peter. He became certain, bold, trustworthy, and able. He emerged as a leader and led the other apostles to testify fearlessly as eyewitnesses of the resurrection.

Are you certain of the resurrection of Jesus? Have you examined the evidence of the resurrection to allow it to embolden your own confidence? If not, review the case for the resurrection in *Cold-Case Christianity* or *Alive*.

Acts 1:6–8

So when they had come together, they were asking Him, saying, "Lord, is it at this time You are restoring the kingdom to Israel?" He said to them, "It is not for you to know times or epochs which the Father has fixed by His own authority; but you will receive power when the Holy Spirit has come upon you; and you shall be My *witnesses* both in Jerusalem, and in all Judea and Samaria, and even to the remotest part of the earth."

The people who knew Jesus personally, those who observed His miracles and heard His teaching, eventually made the case based on their authority as *eyewitnesses*. Before Jesus ascended into heaven, He told His disciples to go and "make disciples of all the nations, baptizing them in the name of the Father and the Son and the Holy Spirit, teaching them to observe all that I commanded you."[12] Jesus's followers then took a very distinctive approach as they evangelized unbelievers. While a variety of evangelism programs have emerged in the church over the years, the first disciples didn't employ any of the techniques and strategies we sometimes use today. Relying on their evidential status as eyewitnesses, the apostles acted as commission case makers. In nearly every encounter with nonbelievers, the apostles began by simply sharing what they saw with their own eyes. Look at Peter's first sermon at Pentecost, for example:

Acts 2:23–24, 32

This man [Jesus] was handed over to you by God's set purpose and foreknowledge; and you, with the help of wicked men, put him to death by nailing him to the cross. But God raised him from the dead, freeing him from the agony of death, because it was impossible for death to keep its

Forensic Faith Profile:

JOHN, SON OF ZEBEDEE

Jesus called John and his older brother, James, the "sons of thunder," based on the zeal they occasionally demonstrated (see Mark 9:38 and Luke 9:54) as passionate defenders of the truth. John revealed his zeal for truth and case making in his own gospel where he used evidential language more than any other gospel author and testified to the evidence of Jesus's miracles. John cited these miracles repeatedly as evidence of Jesus's deity. Interestingly, John is traditionally recognized as the "disciple whom Jesus loved" (John 13:23). He was most likely the youngest of Jesus's disciples, yet he possessed great boldness that endeared the affection of his Master.

God can use youthful passion and boldness. Are there young believers in your life? How have you been equipping them to defend the truth? Is there someone in particular you could mentor and prepare?

hold on him … God has raised this Jesus to life, and *we are all witnesses* of the fact.

In the days and months following Peter's first sermon, he and the other apostles continued to take this straightforward case-making approach to evangelism. They relied on the direct evidence of their testimony as eyewitnesses:

Peter's second sermon, as recorded in Acts 3:15:
You killed the author of life, but God raised him from the dead. We are *witnesses* of this.

Peter and John, as recorded in Acts 4:20:
We cannot help speaking about *what we have seen and heard.*

All the apostles, as recorded in Acts 4:33:
With great power the apostles *continued to testify to the resurrection of the Lord Jesus.* And God's grace was so powerfully at work in them all.

Peter, as recorded in Acts 10:39–42:
We are witnesses of everything he [Jesus] did in the country of the Jews and in Jerusalem. They killed him by hanging him on a cross, but God raised him from the dead on the third day and caused him to be seen. He was not seen by all the people, but by witnesses whom God had already chosen—by us who ate and drank with him after he rose from the dead. He commanded us to preach to the people and to *testify* that he is the one whom God appointed as judge of the living and the dead.

Paul, as recorded in Acts 17:2–3:
And according to Paul's custom, he went to them, and for three Sabbaths reasoned with them from the Scriptures, *explaining and giving evidence* that

the Christ had to suffer and rise again from the dead, and saying, "This Jesus whom I am proclaiming to you is the Christ."

Paul, as recorded in Acts 17:30–31:
Therefore having overlooked the times of ignorance, God is now declaring to men that all people everywhere should repent, because He has fixed a day in which He will judge the world in righteousness through a Man whom He has appointed, *having furnished proof to all men* by raising Him from the dead.

Given all the possible ways they could have shared the message of the gospel, the apostles chose to make the case based on the evidence of their own observations. The first hearers of the apostles came to faith on the basis of this evidential approach. If you're a Christian today, evidence also played a critical role in your conversion, even if you weren't aware of it at the time. If someone shared scripture with you or told you about Jesus as He was described in the New Testament, they were relying on the *eyewitness* observations and descriptions of the *apostles*, just like Jesus described in His prayer in John's gospel (chapter 17). God sovereignly calls us to Himself, communicating His truth with *direct evidence*. Blessed are we who did not see and yet believed the *testimony of the eyewitnesses*.

Christ
the Case Maker

The Commissioned
Case Makers

The Rich, Evidential History of Christian Case-Making

FORENSIC FAITH EVIDENTIAL EXAMPLE #3:
THE CANONICAL CASE MAKERS

The writers of Scripture understood the evidential, case-making importance of their eyewitness authority. In fact, the authors of the Gospels *relied* on this authority to make their case. The apostle John, for example, closed his gospel by referencing his status as an eyewitness:

John 21:24–25

This is the disciple who is *testifying* to these things and wrote these things, and we know that his *testimony* is true. And there are also many other things which Jesus did, which if they were written in detail, I suppose that even the world itself would not contain the books that would be written.

Even Luke, who would later write a comprehensive history of the life, ministry, death, and resurrection of Jesus, understood the value and authority of the original witnesses. In the opening lines of his gospel, he told his readers he was relying on the testimony of eyewitnesses:

Luke 1:1–4

Inasmuch as many have undertaken to compile an account of the things accomplished among us, just as they

Forensic Faith Profile:
PAUL OF TARSUS

Paul (also known by his Hebrew name, Saul) was raised as a devout Jew (a Pharisee) and trained at the school of one of the most famous rabbis in history (Gamaliel). In his position of leadership and authority, he hunted Christian believers and "brought them bound to Jerusalem" (see Acts 22:5). In spite of his stubborn intellectual and religious commitments, Paul's life was forever changed when he became an eyewitness to the risen Christ on the road to Damascus. His own personal observations of Jesus convinced him of the truth. He became a follower of Jesus and went on to write fourteen books of the New Testament.

Even those of us who were adamantly opposed to God can be transformed by the evidence. Can you think of a steadfast nonbeliever in your life? Have you shared the evidence for Christianity with him or her? Have you talked to this person long enough to discover the intellectual objections he or she might have?

were *handed down to us by those who from the beginning were eyewitnesses and servants of the word*, it seemed fitting for me as well, having investigated everything carefully from the beginning, to write it out for you in consecutive order, most excellent Theophilus; so that you may know the exact truth about the things you have been taught.

Evidence mattered to the earliest believers. They trusted the accounts offered by John and Matthew because these men knew Jesus personally. These disciples provided direct evidence (eyewitness testimony) in their gospels. Luke's gospel was embraced by the early church on the basis of Luke's evidential, investigative approach. Luke interviewed the eyewitnesses and included their testimony. Even Mark's gospel was accepted based on its eyewitness value. While Mark may not have known Jesus personally, his gospel, according to the first-century bishop Papias of Hierapolis, was the accurate collection of testimony from an important eyewitness, Simon Peter.[13] The apostles (and the men who wrote about them) understood their evidential, case-making role in the earliest Christian communities.

The gospel authors weren't the only authors of Scripture who understood the importance of their eyewitness status. Paul, for example, continually referred to his own encounter with Jesus to establish the authenticity of his office and writings. Paul also directed his readers to other eyewitnesses who could corroborate his claims:

1 Corinthians 15:3–8

For I delivered to you as of first importance what I also received, that Christ died for our sins according to the Scriptures, and that He was buried, and that He was raised on the third day according to the Scriptures, and that *He appeared to Cephas, then to the twelve*. After that *He appeared to more than five hundred brethren at one time*, most of whom remain until now, but some have fallen asleep; then *He appeared to James, then to all the apostles*; and last of all, as to one untimely born, *He appeared to me also*.

Paul built his case on the *indirect* evidence of the Old Testament prophecies, confirmed by the *direct* evidence of eyewitnesses who saw the prophecies fulfilled. As an eyewitness of the risen

Christ, he understood the power of eyewitness testimony. The evidential authors of the other New Testament epistles also identified themselves as eyewitnesses when writing to members of the church:

1 Peter 5:1

Therefore, I exhort the elders among you, as your fellow elder and *witness of the sufferings of Christ*, and a partaker also of the glory that is to be revealed.

2 Peter 1:16

For we did not follow cleverly devised tales when we made known to you the power and coming of our Lord Jesus Christ, but we were *eyewitnesses* of His majesty.

1 John 1:1–3

What was from the beginning, what we have heard, what we have seen with our eyes, what we have looked at and touched with our hands, concerning the Word of Life—and the life was manifested, and we have seen and testify and proclaim to you the eternal life, which was with the Father and was manifested to us—*what we have seen and heard* we proclaim to you also, so that you too may have fellowship with us.

The New Testament canon of Scripture was written by men who understood their evidential, case-making role. As they approached the ends of their lives, they made sure they left us with a written record of everything they observed and learned so we could also someday make the case.

Christ
the Case Maker

The Commissioned
Case Makers

The Canonical
Case Makers

The Rich, Evidential History of Christian Case-Making

FORENSIC FAITH EVIDENTIAL EXAMPLE #4:
THE CONTINUING CASE MAKERS

Christian history is filled with Christians who made the case based on what the canonical case makers provided on the pages of the New Testament. If there's one consistent leadership thread throughout the history of the church, it's the continuing influence of Christian case makers. After the ascension of Jesus and the deaths of those who were eyewitnesses, early Christians continued to make the case. Here are just a few early "standouts":

Quadratus of Athens (ca. AD 60–129)

The earliest believers didn't hesitate to make the case for Christianity. Quadratus was a disciple of the apostles. He wrote to Emperor Hadrian in an effort to respond to accusations made against the early church. Making the case for the truth of Christianity, Quadratus offered, as evidence, the existence of people healed by Jesus who were still alive in Quadratus's day.

> **Forensic Faith Definition:**
> ## EVANGELIST
>
> Derived from the Greek word *euaggelizó* (εὐαγγελίζω), an evangelist is someone who "brings good news." While early Greek texts used the term to describe the four authors of the Gospels, the word was also applied to anyone who first brought the gospel (the good news of Jesus) to a city, region, or people group.
>
> Want to be an evangelist? You'll need two things: First you'll need to grasp the outrageous free gift of salvation through Jesus, who forgives our sins and purifies us from all unrighteousness (1 John 1:9). Are you excited about this good news? Second, you'll need a group, region, or person who hasn't yet heard the gospel. Who in your life has yet to fully comprehend the nature of forgiveness and the gift of salvation?

Aristides of Athens (ca. AD 70–134)

This Athenian philosopher also wrote a defense of Christianity for Emperor Hadrian. He made his case by comparing the worldviews of four cultures well known to the emperor, highlighting the superiority of Christian claims about God and the resulting lifestyles of Christians. He referenced the Gospels as eyewitness accounts and encouraged the emperor to respond to his case and become a Christian.

Ariston of Pella (ca. AD 100–160)

Known as a case maker and "chronicler," Ariston is the first Christian known to make a written defense for Christianity against Jewish objections. His work took the form of a written dialogue between a Christian and Jewish believer in which the Christian character made the case using messianic prophecies from the Old Testament and demonstrating how Jesus fulfilled those prophecies.

Justin Martyr (ca. AD 100–165)

Born into a pagan family, Justin Martyr identified himself as a Gentile. He authored many important case-making documents, including two in which he made the case for Christianity to Emperor Antoninus Pius and the Roman Senate. Justin sought to reconcile the claims of faith and reason for his readers and argued that traces of the truth ("seeds of Christianity") could even be found in the writings of historical Greek philosophers who predated Jesus.

Apollinaris Claudius (ca. AD 100–175)

Apollinaris Claudius became famous as a case maker, defending the truth of Christianity to Emperor Marcus Aurelius and making the case against early heretics in the church. Apollinaris cited the evidence of answered prayer when arguing for the truth of Christianity with the emperor.

Tertullian (ca. AD 155–240)

Quintus Septimius Florens Tertullianus was a prolific Christian case maker. He wrote to defend the church against heresy and also made the case for the triune nature of God. Tertullian wrote *Apologeticus* to the magistrates in Rome, in which he made the case for Christianity and argued that freedom of religion was an inalienable human right.

Marcus Minucius Felix (ca. AD 180–250)

Born in Africa, this case maker authored *Octavius*, a fictional dialogue between a Christian and a pagan. Felix used this dialogue to respond to common objections leveled against Christianity at the time, while making a sophisticated case for monotheism.

If you're a fan of Christian history, there's a good chance your favorite Christian case maker isn't mentioned in my brief list. We could easily fill this book with hundreds of fascinating stories of Christianity's historic defenders, but that's not my goal. Instead, I want to illustrate the continuous case-making attitude that permeated ancient believers who were most directly influenced by Jesus and His apostles.

| Christ the Case Maker | The Commissioned Case Makers | The Canonical Case Makers | The Continuing Case Makers |

The Rich, Evidential History of Christian Case-Making

FORENSIC FAITH EVIDENTIAL EXAMPLE #5:
THE CONTEMPORARY CASE MAKERS

Case making was important to these early believers, and it ought to be just as important to those of us who follow these men. We've also been commanded to share what we believe as Christians. Maybe that's why we often feel convicted about our lack of zeal when it comes to evangelism. Not many of us are consistent evangelists.

The New Testament seems to present us with a paradox. On the one hand, we're given a Great Commission to share the gospel and make disciples. Paul, however, seemed to recognize that not everyone is an evangelist:

Ephesians 4:11–13

And He gave *some* as apostles, and *some* as prophets, and *some* as evangelists, and *some* as pastors and teachers, for the equipping of the saints for the work of service, to the building up of the body of Christ; until we all attain to the unity of the faith, and of the knowledge of the Son of God, to a mature man, to the measure of the stature which belongs to the fullness of Christ.

Paul repeatedly said some of us are designed and given to perform certain functions. *Some* are apostles, *some* are prophets, *some* are evangelists, *some* are teachers, and *some* are pastors. Think about that for a minute. The reasonable inference here is that some of us *are* given to function in this way, and some of us *are not.* You may be gifted and given by God to be a pastor, or you may not. In a similar way, you may not be an *evangelist.*

How, then, are we all supposed to engage the Great Commission if only *some* of us are evangelists? The apostle Peter provided us with an answer. As it turns out, there's another "Great Commission calling" we ought to feel on our lives as Christians, one that we usually ignore altogether. Let's return to what Peter said in his letter written to "exiles scattered throughout the provinces of Pontus, Galatia, Cappadocia, Asia and Bithynia":

1 Peter 3:15–16

But in your hearts set apart Christ as Lord. Always be prepared to *give an answer* to everyone who asks you

Forensic Faith Definition:
CHRISTIAN CASE MAKER

The Christian term *apologist* can be confusing to nonbelievers and believers alike. Are Christians who study apologetics trying to learn how to apologize? No. The term *Christian case maker* correctly characterizes the essence of the Greek word *apologia* (ἀπολογία) and describes our duty to make the case for what we believe with gentleness and respect.

If you've been calling yourself a Christian, how would the new label, Christian case maker, change the way you think about your identity, duty, and responsibility as a Christ follower?

to give the reason for the hope that you have. But do this with gentleness and respect, keeping a clear conscience, so that those who speak maliciously against your good behavior in Christ may be ashamed of their slander.

Peter used an interesting word here when he told these believers to "give an answer." The word in Greek is *apologia* (ἀπολογία). It means something akin to "giving a well-reasoned reply" or "providing a thoughtful response to a question offered." *Apologia* has nothing to do with being remorseful or *apologetic*. Instead, it simply describes our duty to "make the case" for what we believe. The word is used (in one form or another) seventeen times in the New Testament (Luke 12:11; 21:14; Acts 19:33; 22:1; 24:10; 25:8; 25:15; 26:1–2, 24; Romans 2:15; 1 Corinthians 9:3; 2 Corinthians 7:11; 12:19; Philippians 1:7; 1:17; and 2 Timothy 4:16). *Apologia* is used most often in the context of some form of *persecution* on the part of believers (as Peter used it here when addressing Christ followers who had been dispersed into regions filled with hostile nonbelievers).

Peter was unequivocal in his directive to these Christ followers. Unlike Paul, who clearly said *not everyone* is an *evangelist*, Peter made a point to say *everyone* must be a *case maker,* particularly when living in a hostile environment. Peter's words apply to *all of us*. It's time for each and every one of us to accept our duty and calling as *Christian case makers.*

| Christ the Case Maker | The Commissioned Case Makers | The Canonical Case Makers | The Continuing Case Makers | The Contemporary Case Makers |

The Rich, Evidential History of Christian Case-Making

THE COMING CASE MAKERS

To this point, I've been arguing for Christian case making from the evidence of the *past*. Now let me take a minute to argue for Christian case making from my expectations of the *future*. We're in a growingly hostile environment. Fewer Americans identify themselves as Christians than ever before, more young Christians are walking away from the church than in prior generations, Christian values are more fervently under attack, and atheistic skepticism is more vocal and intense. The trajectory doesn't favor Christianity, at least here in America. There's another group of Christians in the diagram I've been unveiling in this chapter: our children and grandchildren. Our parents' generation was far *less* opposed to the church and the claims of Christianity than ours is today, but our children's generation will be far *more* opposed.

Three generations of Jim Wallaces learned the importance of reason and evidence. This tradition was passed down from generation to generation until it became a part of our family identity. If my son, Jimmy, has a child, there might be a fourth Jim Wallace to continue the law enforcement tradition. If that happens, it will be my son's responsibility to pass on the values and responsibilities he learned from me. If we hope to prepare the next generation of *Christians* for the upcoming challenge, we need to pass on the values and responsibilities we've learned from those who came before us. We must show our children what Christian case making looks like. We need to embrace and model a *forensic faith*.

WHAT IS FORENSIC FAITH?

We have a duty to know *what* we believe and *why* we believe it so we can give an answer, contend for the faith, and model Christian case making for the next generation of believers. Are you ready? If someone challenged you with a few simple objections, could you make a case for what you believe?

The adjective *forensic* comes from the Latin word *forensis*, which means "in open court" or "public." The term usually refers to the process detectives and prosecutors use to investigate and establish evidence in a public trial or debate. You seldom hear the word attached to our traditional notions of "faith," but given what I've already described in this chapter, it seems particularly appropriate when describing the kind of faith Jesus expected from His followers. Jesus did not affirm the notion of "blind faith," and He didn't ask us to believe something unsupported by the evidence. Consider the following definitions of "faith":

Unreasonable Faith

Believing in something *in spite* of the evidence.

We hold an unreasonable belief when we refuse to accept or acknowledge evidence that clearly *refutes* what we think is true. The claim "touching a toad will cause warts" is an excellent example. We now have evidence that viruses, not toads or frogs, cause warts, so people who still believe you can contract warts from toads hold an unreasonable belief. In a similar way, *unreasonable faith* results in believing in something *false* (because it can be disproved by the evidence). Jesus did not ask His followers to ignore the world around them or to ignore evidence that might refute His claims. In fact, to this day, there *isn't* any evidence disproving the eyewitness accounts recorded in the Gospels.

Blind Faith

Believing in something *without* any evidence.

We hold a blind belief when we accept a claim even though we are completely unaware of any evidence supporting the claim. I believe, for example, that James David Wallace Sr. is my biological father, even though I am unaware of any DNA test results that would prove this definitively. I may be right about our biological relationship, or I may be wrong; I would only know for sure if I were to perform a paternity test. In a similar way, blind faith can sometimes result in believing something that's *true*, but it can also result in believing something that's *false* if there is actual evidence proving the claim untrue. Jesus did not ask His followers to believe without evidence. In fact, He repeatedly provided evidence to support His claims.

Forensic Faith

Believing in something *because* of the evidence.

We hold a forensic belief when we believe something because it is the most reasonable inference from evidence, even though we may still have some unanswered questions. I believe, for example, that amoxicillin can help fight bacterial infections. There is laboratory evidence to support this claim, and I've personally used it to fight infections. I still don't know how (or why) this drug works, but I have faith in amoxicillin, even though I have many unanswered questions. In a similar way, Jesus encouraged us to have a *forensic faith* based on the evidence

He provided. He knew we would still have unanswered questions, but He wanted us to be able to defend what we believe (and guard the truth) in a hostile public setting.

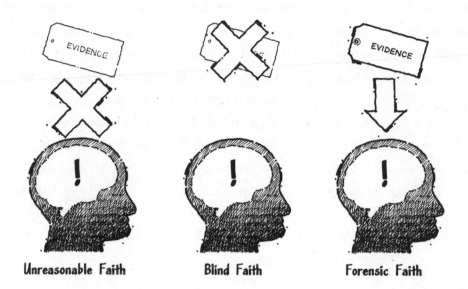

If you're like me, you have friends who embrace one of these three categories of faith. In fact, you may even recognize *yourself* somewhere in this list. I've certainly been in a couple of these categories over the course of my life. When I was an atheist, I believed the universe and everything in it could be explained by (and with) nothing more than space, time, matter, and the laws that govern such things. But I had to ignore the evidence and accept insufficient atheistic explanations for the complex information in the genetic code, the fine-tuning in the universe, the appearance of design in biology, and the existence of nonmaterial minds and mental free agency (more on this in *God's Crime Scene*). Despite evidence to the contrary, I continued to trust my naturalistic view of the world was actually *true*. I believed this *in spite of* the evidence; I held an *unreasonable faith*.

I was hesitant to consider Christianity, however, because the few Christians I knew seemed to hold a completely unexamined faith; they hadn't investigated the evidence *at all*. They simply trusted Christianity was true on the basis of their upbringing or their own interpretation of personal, private experiences. Now before I go any further, let me make something very clear: I do believe in what some Christians call the "inner witness of the Holy Spirit." In other words, I believe the experiences Christians have when convicted by the Holy Spirit are, in fact, important pieces of *evidence*. But given that my Mormon family *also* cited spiritual confirmation of this sort, I was hesitant to accept these experiences as conclusive *proof*. After all, everyone can cite *some* sort of religious experience. As a detective, I needed something to differentiate between the competing claims of the believers I knew. From my perspective, both my Christian friends and my Mormon family members believed something *without* corroborative evidence; they had *blind faith* in their own personal experiences.

As I began to read the New Testament for myself, I realized there was a distinctly Christian *faith alternative*. Based on my limited experience with Christians, I assumed blind faith was a Christian *requirement*. The New Testament proved me wrong. I was repeatedly encouraged and surprised by the evidential approach taken by Jesus, the apostles, and the writers of the New Testament. Although some Christians may believe Christianity is true without any evidence, Jesus never required this. Instead, Jesus asked His followers to believe *because of* the evidence; as Christians, we ought to have a *forensic faith*.

IF WE ARE RELYING ON EVIDENCE, WHY CALL IT FAITH?

Forensic Faith Challenge:

FAITH IS INCOMPATIBLE WITH REASON

Skeptics in our culture often argue faith is the *opposite* of reason. They also typically characterize themselves as the only "reasonable" people in the debate. How would you respond to this common objection given what you now know about the evidential nature of Christianity? Can you think of two or three things you might say to someone who makes this kind of claim?

For a suggested response and resources to help you answer similar objections, see the Rebuttal Notes section.

Now you might be saying, "If you believe something *because of the evidence*, why use the word *faith* at all?" Juries render verdicts on the basis of the evidence and we don't call their decisions an act of "faith," do we? If evidence is an integral part of "faith decisions," what is left for there to have "faith" about?

In all the years I've spent in criminal trials, I've yet to investigate or present a case in which there wasn't a number of questions the jury simply could *not* answer. Although my cases are typically robust, cumulative, and compelling, they always have some informational *limit*. A recent case was an excellent example; jurors convicted the defendant even though they couldn't answer the following questions: How precisely did the defendant dispose of the victim's body? How did he find time to clean up the crime scene? What did he do with the murder weapon? How did he move the victim's car without being seen?

Some questions simply cannot be answered unless a suspect is willing to confess to the crime (and that doesn't happen often). The existence of unanswered (and *unanswerable*) questions is such a common part of jury trials that prosecutors typically ask jurors (prior to their selection) if they require *every* question be answered before they can render a decision. When potential jurors say they need every question answered, we simply remove them from consideration.

Jurors make decisions even though they have less than complete information, and they aren't the only people who make decisions in this way. Regardless of theistic (or atheistic) worldview, we all trust something is true, even though we can't answer all the questions. Today, I am a Christian because the evidence for God's existence and the reliability of the New Testament are robust, cumulative, and compelling. This doesn't mean all my questions are answered. They aren't. But I've reached a conclusion based on the evidence I *do* have in much the same way a jury reaches a decision. In a strict sense, this is actually an "act of faith," given that I trust in something I can't fully demonstrate or understand. But my "faith decision" is more akin to "trusting in the best inference from the evidence" than "believing blindly" or "believing in something in spite of the evidence."

BUT WHY MAKE THE CASE, IF GOD IS IN CONTROL?

You might also be wondering, depending on your theological position as a Christian, if this evidential approach to Christian belief is necessary if God is sovereign and is solely responsible for calling believers to Himself. If God calls His chosen, can't He achieve this without any case-making effort on our part? I also pondered this question as a new Christian, and I think the following analogy is helpful, although certainly imperfect.

When my son David was a young boy, he hated mushrooms. If salvation were dependent on voluntarily ordering a mushroom pizza, David would never experience heaven because he would never, on his own accord, order such a pizza. In fact, I once took David to a pizza restaurant and cleverly removed the mushrooms from a pizza in an effort to convince him to eat it. He refused. "I can see the shape of the mushroom right there!" He knew it had been poisoned by "mushroom juice," and no amount of effort on my part could change his mind, in spite of my best mushroom-pizza case-making efforts.

But what if there was some way to remove David's hatred of mushrooms *prior* to entering the restaurant? If David no longer hated mushrooms, he would be open to my mushroom-pizza case-making efforts. Then, if I was able to make a "five-point case for the deliciousness of mushroom pizza," David would, under his new nature (having had his hatred for mushrooms removed), choose to voluntarily order the mushroom pizza.

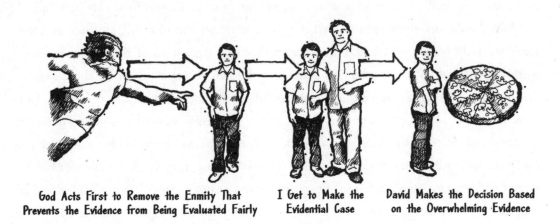

God Acts First to Remove the Enmity That   I Get to Make the   David Makes the Decision Based
Prevents the Evidence from Being Evaluated Fairly   Evidential Case   on the Overwhelming Evidence

In this admittedly imperfect analogy, David's salvation was clearly dependent *first* on the role God played in removing his enmity for mushrooms. But once this enmity was sovereignly lifted, David was open to my case making. God allowed me to play my role as a case maker, and David responded to my effort in a way he never would have if God hadn't first moved.

God's incredible love for us is evident in this process. God loved my son enough to remove his hostility, and He loved me enough to disciple and encourage me. Even though God is clearly sovereign, He graciously allowed me to play a part in reaching David. I got to make the case for what I know is true about salvation, and in the process, my confidence grew as I mastered the evidence for Christianity. God's sovereign purposes and amazing love were ultimately expressed both in the son He called and in the son He encouraged.

IT'S OUR DUTY

After the graduation ceremony, my family assembled in front of the Civic Center and took pictures on the lawn. My grandfather Warner couldn't stop smiling. My father pinned a new badge on my uniform. In that moment, as I stood next to my dad wearing the same uniform I'd seen him wear my entire life, I knew I was part of an important team. I was acutely aware of my duty, my family obligation, and my mission. I had just sworn to support and defend the constitution of my state and country from all enemies, and I pledged to protect my community. Although we just completed sixteen weeks of training at the academy, more targeted training was about to begin. Over the next twenty-five years, I would learn how to conduct investigations and communicate the truth convincingly. The hard work was about to begin anew, but I was eager to accept the challenge.

If you're a Christian, you're part of an even more important team. You have a duty, a family obligation, and a mission.

> **Forensic Faith Assignment:**
> ## FIND YOUR PLACE
> Every officer on our SWAT, surveillance, and homicide teams knows his or her role. We usually find our place by recognizing our unique gifts and passions. Given my love of communication and the arts, I was called into service every time a suspect needed to be interviewed or a diagram needed to be drawn.
>
> What are your unique gifts and interests? Where can you be the most effective case maker? What group can you reach, given your work background or special interests?

You're called to embrace a forensic faith so you can make the case for what you believe and contend for the faith. Now it's time to begin some targeted training so you can learn how to investigate the case and communicate it to others. It's time to learn the difference between *teaching* and *training*.

Chapter Two
TARGETED TRAINING
5 Steps toward Preparing Yourself to Protect and Serve as a First Responder

> *"Now the true soldiers of Christ must always be prepared to do battle for the truth, and must never, so far as lies with them, allow false convictions to creep in."[1]*
>
> Origen

> *"Train up a child in the way he should go—but be sure you go that way yourself."*
>
> Charles Spurgeon

"Man down, man down! Holster your weapons!"

I knew I had been hit several times. My right arm and chest were stinging, and I could see my uniform shirt was covered in red. I was more embarrassed than injured, however.

I was a new member of SWAT and the least tenured officer on the team. Although I considered myself a good shot, my opponent was a much better, more seasoned marksman. His uniform was unblemished, while mine (including my ballistic helmet) was speckled with red paint.

We were training in an abandoned elementary school that had been scheduled for demolition. We spent weeks in the facility prior to the arrival of the bulldozers, creating training scenarios that tested our entry teams repeatedly. I can't even remember how many mistakes I made in these sessions—many more than I care to admit, for sure. But the experience was worth it.

In the early days of training, I was continually peppered with red paint from the paintball pistols we used. The marksman playing the barricaded suspect consistently won these early battles, and I seldom hit him in return. But as the training progressed, my tactics improved, and I ultimately mastered my position on the team. The more we trained, the less I had to wash my uniforms.

Training is essential in law enforcement because officers deploy on a regular basis. If we could handle every call over the phone without leaving the station, none of us would need to exercise or train tactically. You don't have to *train* if you have no intention of *deploying*. The same is true for us as Christians. Think about that for a minute. Most of us see our church buildings as places to gather on Sunday; seldom do we think of them as places to *train* in preparation for *deployment*. As long as our experience *as the church* is limited to meeting *in a church* (building), there's little reason to engage in meaningful training. We need to rethink our *role* so we can rethink our *response*.

Forensic Faith Definition:
DEPLOY

Deploy, from the Latin word *desplicare* (meaning "to scatter"), describes the act of organizing and sending out people (or things) for a *particular purpose*. As Christians, God wants us to engage the culture as an act of deployment. We can do this either willingly or unwillingly. In Acts 11:19, Luke described how God used the persecution of Christians in Jerusalem to accomplish an important deployment: "Those who were scattered because of the persecution that occurred in connection with Stephen made their way to Phoenicia and Cyprus and Antioch, speaking the word." If we aren't willing to deploy *voluntarily*, God may deploy us in a more dramatic fashion.

Looking back at your own life, can you think of a circumstance in which God may have been trying to "scatter" you into an important mission field? Where have you been deployed today, and are you accomplishing the particular purpose God intended for your deployment?

THEIR MOTTO IS ALSO OUR MOTTO

If we are going to adopt the Los Angeles Police motto, we'll need to understand and accept our role as servants and protectors. If what we believe about Christianity is *true*, it's our obligation to serve others by sharing the truth with them. If eternity hangs in the balance and our destiny rests on the central truth claims of the Christian worldview, what kind of people would we be if we let our friends and neighbors spend their eternal lives separated from God?

Christians have a rich tradition of service, establishing hospitals, soup kitchens, and shelters for the homeless. We serve the *physical* needs of people in our community (by demonstrating the *love* of Christ) so we can meet their *spiritual* needs (by sharing the *truth* of Christ). Christians, therefore, proclaim the gospel in two distinct ways: with our words and with our actions. Our deeds of service allow us the opportunity to demonstrate the love of God as we proclaim the good news of Jesus Christ.

Like officers, Christians are called to *protect*. The truth of Christianity is the cure for what's killing all of us; it's the very source of spiritual life. Like all important cures, the purity of Christian truth claims must be protected. A *contaminated cure* can be *poisonous*. When Jesus met the Samaritan woman at the well (in John 4:7–30), for example, He offered her "living water." But water is of little value if it is contaminated. In fact, contaminated water has been responsible for death since ancient times. Purity is critical to the life-giving value of water, and in a similar way, purity is critical to the life-giving claims of Christianity. If the Christian message is contaminated, distorted, or amended, it ceases to be the Christian message. Like poison, a corrupted gospel leads to death. That's why the apostles were so adamant about our role as *guardians of truth*. When saying good-bye to the believers in Ephesus, Paul challenged the Ephesians to guard and protect themselves from error:

Acts 20:27–31

For I did not shrink from declaring to you the whole purpose of God. Be *on guard* for yourselves and for all the flock, among which the Holy Spirit has made you overseers, to shepherd the church of God which He purchased with His own blood. I know that after my departure savage wolves will come in among you, not sparing the flock; and from among your own selves men will arise, speaking perverse things, to draw away the disciples after them. Therefore be on the alert.

Paul wasn't writing exclusively to *leaders* (although he did similarly admonish Timothy as a leader in 1 Timothy 6:20–21); Paul was writing to *every* member of the church in Ephesus, regardless of their leadership role. Peter also understood the importance of protecting the truth. He commanded his readers to treat the truth with great respect and guard it against opposition from outside *and inside* the church:

Forensic Faith Definition:
COMMITMENT

While most of us, as Christians, want to be committed to the cause of Christ, commitment, by definition, is more than simply "a promise to be loyal to someone or something." It is also "a promise to do or give something."[2] Our commitment must be more than intellectual or verbal. True commitment results in action.

In what areas of your life would a casual observer readily agree your actions are consistent with your Christian commitment? Are there places where you could improve your commitment by fulfilling your promise to do something in the name of Christ?

2 Peter 3:14–18

Therefore, beloved, since you look for these things, be diligent to be found by Him in peace, spotless and blameless, and regard the patience of our Lord as salvation; just as also our beloved brother Paul, according to the wisdom given him, wrote to you, as also in all his letters, speaking in them of these things, in which are some things hard to understand, which the untaught and unstable distort, as they do also the rest of the Scriptures, to their own destruction. You therefore, beloved, knowing this beforehand, *be on your guard* so that you are not carried away by the error of unprincipled men and fall from your own steadfastness, but grow in the grace and knowledge of our Lord and Savior Jesus Christ.

Once again, Peter wasn't writing exclusively to church leaders; he was addressing *every* member of the Christian family. It's our common obligation to protect and guard the truth claims of Christianity. The Los Angeles Police motto is also our motto as Christians. We are called to serve and to protect.

Now, more than ever, we need to *serve* those who have not yet heard the gospel and *protect* those who have. The secular culture is more *aggressive* and the Christian culture is more *vulnerable* than ever before. A recent Barna Group poll revealed that only 9 percent of American adults possess a biblical worldview, acknowledging the existence of objective moral truth, asserting the accuracy of the Bible, believing in the existence of Satan, understanding the relationship between grace and "works," affirming the sinless life of Jesus, and comprehending the classic attributes of God.[3] Worse yet, only 19 percent of self-professing *Christians* were found to hold a biblical worldview. In another survey, Barna found that younger generations of Americans are less likely to believe Jesus is God, and Christians are increasingly divided about the sinless character of Jesus and the nature of salvation.[4]

All this is happening as the church continues to teach its members as it always has. In broad sections of our country, traditional Sunday school classes and programs are still in place and an important part of church culture. Other less traditional churches have employed midweek services, small groups, life groups, home fellowship groups, cell groups, and a variety of other models to teach Christians the classic truths of Christianity. But the numbers don't lie. Few Christians actually understand what Christianity teaches, and even fewer young Christians can articulate what they believe.[5] All this *teaching* doesn't seem to be making a difference. Maybe it's time for a change.

STOP TEACHING

I wasn't a Christian very long before I was asked to teach my sons' third-grade Sunday school class. I didn't know much at the time, and I was only inches ahead of the students I taught and led every week. Fortunately, we had excellent curricula, and I learned quickly. I eventually entered Golden Gate Baptist Theological Seminary and earned a seminary degree. By the time I graduated, I was serving as a high school youth pastor. I'll never forget my first year with junior and senior high schoolers. It was mostly a train wreck. I struggled to find my voice and understand my mission, and after graduating the first group of seniors, I discovered that all but one had walked away from their faith by winter break of their freshman year in college. I was shocked, and I felt like a complete failure.

In that first year, I focused on my gifting as an artist and musician rather than my skill set as a detective. I was a design major prior to entering law enforcement, and I received my master's degree in architecture from UCLA before I entered the police academy. As a new youth pastor, I exercised this gifting and created weekly "experiences" for my students. Music, imagery, and environment were important to me as I walked through the Scripture with my group. The ministry grew quickly, and it seemed successful, at least by the metrics we often use to measure success. But once I realized our graduating seniors were no longer Christians, I knew I had to shift gears. Something had to change, and I knew precisely what it was. We needed to *stop teaching*.

> **Forensic Faith Definition:**
> ## TRAINING
> To *train* is "to make proficient by instruction and practice, as in some art, profession, or work."[6] Training is more than mere instruction. Training involves putting instruction into *practice*.
>
> Have you been putting what you've learned as a Christian into practice? If not, why not? What are the obstacles standing in your path? How might you overcome these obstacles? What priorities would have to change for you to make training a real part of your Christian faith?

In the years since making this change, I've given the same advice to many other youth pastors, church leaders, and parents. *Stop teaching your young people.* We've got lots of great teachers in the church and lots of concerned parents who want to teach their kids. We've been teaching young people for generations. But this teaching has obviously become ineffective, if the current statistics related to the departure rates of young people in their college years are even remotely accurate. We've been *teaching*, and students have been *leaving*. It's time to stop *teaching* and start *training*.

Don't get me wrong; I recognize the biblical importance of *teaching*. Paul, for example, affirmed the instructive value of Scripture in one of his letters to Timothy:

> **2 Timothy 3:16**
>
> All Scripture is inspired by God and profitable for *teaching*, for reproof, for correction.

Paul told Timothy he should use the Scripture to teach, reprove, and correct, but he didn't stop there. Paul identified another important use for God's Word:

> **2 Timothy 3:16–17**
>
> All Scripture is inspired by God and profitable for teaching, for reproof, for correction, for *training* in righteousness; so that the man of God may be adequate, *equipped for every good work*.

Paul made a distinction between *teaching* and *training*. It's time for us to make a distinction as well. We've got to understand the role of *teaching* within the broader context of *training*. Teaching is focused on *imparting knowledge*. Training is focused on *preparing for a challenge* ("equipping" ourselves "for every good work"). Boxers and MMA fighters train. First responders train. Military personnel train. Why? Because they're eventually going to deploy in the ring, in the fighting cage, on the street, or on the battlefield. These people know they're going to be challenged and tested. Unless they prepare for this inevitable reality, they're going to get hurt.

As a young man, I was a boxing *fanatic*. I loved to watch the sport, and I had my favorite boxers. I noticed that even the best of these athletes gained weight, however, in between fights. Like the rest of us, they were sometimes lazy. But once a contract was signed for an upcoming fight, they got serious and started to train, especially in the weeks immediately preceding the bout. Calendared fights typically result in *training*, especially if you want to survive in the ring.

My son Jimmy understands this now that he's a police officer. In his first year on the job, he started training with a well-known local jiujitsu fighter. After the initial session, he came home with a bruise on his forehead. Even though Jimmy was strong and capable, his trainer possessed *specialized* skills. During that first lesson, Jimmy took a beating. I saw him several weeks later and observed he still had fresh injuries on his head and neck. It didn't look like Jimmy was improving. He was quick to tell me otherwise: "It takes him twice as long now to strangle me into submission."

While it may not sound like much, this incremental improvement might someday save Jimmy's life. If Jimmy ever gets in over his head in a wrestling match with a suspect, he'll be able to hold on long enough for his backup to arrive. Sometimes just a few minutes can make all the difference in the world. Jimmy is *training* because he knows the battle is inevitable.

START TRAINING

As Christians, we're going to face our own battles as we try to serve and protect what we believe. It'll be even more difficult for our young people. As leaders and parents, we need to decide whether we're going to face the challenges unprepared or *train* in advance. In my years preparing students, I've learned the difference between teaching and training. I've developed a simple acronym to describe the process:

> **T** – Test
>> Challenge each other to expose our weaknesses.
>
> **R** – Require
>> Expect more from each other than we sometimes think we can handle.
>
> **A** – Arm
>> Learn the truth and how to articulate it.
>
> **I** – Involve
>> Deploy into the battlefield of ideas.
>
> **N** – Nurture
>> Tend to our wounds and model the nature of Jesus.

The challenges facing *young* Christians are simply an amplified version of the challenges facing *all of us*. If we hope to fulfill our duty as Christian case makers, we'll need to rethink our approach to knowledge, information, and education, whether we are leading students, raising kids, or simply becoming better disciples. This training paradigm will prepare us to meet the challenge.

FORENSIC FAITH STEP #1:
TEST YOURSELF AND TEST THOSE YOU LOVE

I've been training students for many years, and I've learned something you can apply to your own personal discipleship effort. Whenever I work with a youth group for an extended period of time, I begin with a *test*. This accomplishes two goals. First, it helps me see where specific weaknesses may be so I can focus my efforts. But more importantly, testing helps all of us understand how much we need to be trained.

My experience as a police officer demonstrated why this is so important. We have a bar in our city that is a constant source of fights and disturbances. Officers are often called to the location to handle difficult problems. It's a perfect place to test new officers. When I was training, my field training officer (FTO) volunteered our unit for any call that was dispatched to this bar because he wanted to see if I could defend myself in a tough situation. At some point, every new officer has to be tested to see if he or she can handle a bar fight, and this bar became the perfect *controlled* test location. I always knew my FTO would be there to cover me if I got in over my head. He wasn't going to let me get hurt. Sometimes I held my own; sometimes I needed his help. After a scuffle in which I didn't fare as well as I would have

Forensic Faith Training:
TEST YOURSELF

There are many ways you can test yourself from the privacy of your own home. Our Forensic Faith Readiness Review is one example. You might also try the following:

There are many videos of debates between theists and atheists on YouTube. Search for these debates and select only those in which the atheist presents *first*. Watch their opening statements and arguments, but stop the videos prior to hearing what the theist has to say in response. Now ask yourself: If you were tasked with answering these atheistic claims, what would you offer in response to his or her objections?

In addition, a simple Internet search will reveal a number of aggressive atheist blogs and websites. Visit these sites, and read what these bloggers have to say. If there are blog posts with comments, read through the comment section, but limit yourself to the statements made by the atheists visiting the blog. Are you ready to respond to the aggressive nature of their objections and claims?

liked, I understood my need for improvement and started training as a fighter and wrestler. I was determined to do better the next time. The *test* exposed my weakness and encouraged me to *train*.

That's why I started testing Christian students in a controlled setting with *role playing*. If at all possible, I try to initially conceal my identity and introduce myself as the *old* Jim, an atheist who has come to discuss what he believes with the group. I spend as much time as possible in this first meeting presenting the case against theism calmly (but unflinchingly) to see if the students (young and old) can defend what they believe. Sadly, they are usually unable to hold their own. These first sessions are typically nerve wracking for Christians who struggle to respond to my claims. My audiences usually begin to squirm anxiously under the weight of dozens of unanswered objections. They don't fare well in this "bar fight." When it's over and I finally reveal I am a Christian who has come to help train them, the relief in the room is *palpable*. They are delighted to see I am a Christian, even though I am obviously aware of the many objections made by atheists, and they are ready and eager to train. In this *controlled* environment, I'm able to reveal their weaknesses without letting them get hurt.

| Once You Know How Much You Don't Know | You'll Know Exactly What You Need To Learn | To Be the Kind of Case-Maker You Need to Be |

Like new officers, there's a time when every Christian, young or old, must be *tested*. We can either seize the opportunity to test in the controlled safety of our ministries, churches, and homes, or we can lose the opportunity and allow the first test to take place in school, in the workplace, or on the streets. It's our choice. If you want to take the next step as a Christian case maker, take a test.

I'd like to offer a simple tool to help you see if you're "ready to make a defense to everyone who asks you to give an account for the hope that is in you." The Forensic Faith Readiness Review is a simple seven-question survey. It's downloadable from our website as a printable PDF file,[7] and it's designed to evaluate your strengths and weaknesses as a Christian case maker. If you don't have access to the website or a printer, you can still evaluate yourself in the following manner:

1. Start with seven lined pieces of notebook paper.

2. Write the following questions at the top of each page (one per page). These questions are designed to reflect the most common questions and objections offered by skeptics:

    a. Why are you a Christian? (Be honest about this response, in spite of what we've already discussed in the preface of this book.)

    b. What evidence do you have to believe God exists?

    c. Why do you trust what the Bible says about Jesus?

    d. Why would God send people to hell just because they don't believe in Jesus?

    e. If God is all-loving and all-powerful, why is there so much evil in the world?

    f. If God is the creator of everything, who created God?

    g. Why would a loving God command the total destruction of all of Israel's enemies (including their children and livestock)?

3. Take three minutes to answer each question before moving on to the next page. Set a timer and do your best to respect these time limits. The entire review should take only twenty-one minutes. Remember, in a real conversation, you may not get much more time than this review allows.

4. After answering the questions, make your own assessment about the answers you've given. Be honest with yourself. Was it difficult to think of a response for each question? Did you struggle to articulate an answer without simply relying on your own subjective experience? While there aren't necessarily "right" or "wrong" answers for each question, some responses are definitely more

persuasive than others. Do you think unbelievers would be satisfied with *your* answers, especially if they asked for objective evidence to support your claims? For a point of comparison, you can refer to the articles linked in the Forensic Faith Readiness Review at ForensicFaithBook.com. (You can also find a set of these article links in the Evidence Locker Section at the end of this book.)

Discover Your Readiness in 21 Minutes

If you're a parent, you can give an abbreviated version of this test to your own children. We've arranged these questions in order of difficulty. Older students are certainly capable of completing the review just as it has been written, but you can shorten the number of questions to suit your own situation. If you think your elementary-aged students are up to it, you might ask them to answer the first three questions, for example, allowing five minutes for each answer. Better yet, ask these questions in an informal way during your next dinner conversation or trip in the car.

This brief Readiness Review will likely open your eyes to your own competency and to the readiness of the young people in your family. Don't be discouraged if you have difficulty answering the questions or are unhappy with the quality of your responses. That's the whole purpose of the review: to form a starting point from which you can begin to grow and improve. These are the kinds of questions skeptics ask and the kinds of questions young Christians struggle to answer. Many young people, when asked why they left the church in their college years, cited the difficulty they had in finding someone in their Christian community or family who could adequately answer similar objections.[8] We need to prepare ourselves with the answers. If we want to grow as believers and make a difference in the lives of young Christians, we need to stop *teaching* and start *training*. It all starts with a test.

FORENSIC FAITH STEP #2:
RAISE THE BAR AND SURPRISE YOURSELF

If you're like me, you've invested many hours training for your profession, preparing for your educational degree, exercising for your personal fitness goals, or even practicing for your favorite hobby. Have you invested the same kind of energy in understanding and defending what you believe as a Christian? We're capable of much more than we typically require of ourselves as believers. The young people in our midst are also far more capable than we typically believe. Many are already engaged in difficult courses of study as they attempt to qualify for universities around the country. Some are taking "honors" courses and "advanced placement" classes. They're willing to work hard when they think there is a need or a tangible goal. Yet when it comes to our expectations in church, we seldom require or challenge ourselves to engage the material with passion, and we rarely express the need for training or set a

Forensic Faith Training:
RAISE THE BAR

How dedicated have you been to preparing yourself as a Christian? What activities and interests have you been placing in front of your effort to make the case for what you believe? Examine the use of your discretionary time. What kinds of sacrifices will you have to make in order to study what you believe?

Make a plan. How much time will you set aside to read, watch, and study? What activities will you need to eliminate to make time for your plan? How soon will you begin?

goal. Once we've tested ourselves and our students, we'll understand our inadequacies and our need for improvement, and when this is clear, we'll be more than willing to do whatever it takes to improve our abilities. We need to raise the bar and require more than ever before.

I've learned to push myself, and I've learned to teach beyond what others may think young Christians can handle. In fact, I teach the material from my two previous books, *Cold-Case Christianity* and *God's Crime Scene*, in precisely the same manner whether I'm teaching a room full of adults or a room full of junior highers. It's the same information-packed presentation, regardless of age group. I never underestimate the ability of my audience, even if they are very young; they can handle whatever I'm teaching if they understand what's at stake.

When I first began my tenure as a youth pastor, my sons and daughters were twelve, ten, five, and four years old. None of them were old enough to be in my ministry, but they chose to sit with me each week as I taught high school students. I was amazed to find how much they understood by the time they were in high school themselves. Even though I was teaching my youth group at a college level, my own elementary-aged children were exposed to everything I said. I was aiming at high school students with high-caliber college-level ammunition, and my elementary children were fortunate to be caught in the crossfire. They benefited from *ricochet apologetics*.

Aim High Because You Never Know What You Might Hit

I want to encourage you to raise the bar and require more of yourself and of those you are discipling. I know it sounds intimidating, but like any worthy, challenging task, it can be accomplished incrementally if you understand the need and are willing to accept the challenge. United States Army Chief of Staff Creighton Abrams once said: "When eating an elephant, take one bite at a time."[9] That's the key to raising the bar: Set a goal and get started. Don't expect to accomplish this overnight. Take small steps, and eventually, you'll be a mile down the road. A year will pass whether you accept this challenge or not. If you require more of yourself and start the journey, you'll exceed your own expectations in that same time frame. You can be a year older and equally unprepared, or a year older and a little bit wiser. Which would you prefer? So, take some time this week and stretch yourself with a book on theology, philosophy of religion, or Christian apologetics. Watch a documentary rather than a sitcom. Embrace the challenge seriously, if not obsessively. Raise the bar, and begin studying the case for Christianity.

FORENSIC FAITH STEP #3:
ARM YOURSELF FOR BATTLE

It would be foolish to dispatch a new police officer into the field without first providing him or her with the tools necessary to do the job. My first Sam Browne equipment belt was filled with pouches containing my handcuffs, extra pistol magazines, mace, and flashlight. There was scarcely room for my holster and baton ring, and I could barely maneuver in and out of my police unit with everything I had to carry. But I felt *equipped*. Better yet, my department trained me to use these tools effectively. I had great tools, and I knew how to use them.

When it comes to equipping ourselves as Christians, the truth is our most effective tool. We need to know the truth and how to use it. Before I taught my children and students the case for Christianity, I taught *myself*. In fact, my lengthy investigation of Christianity was the reason I became a Christian in the first place. I examined the evidence for God's existence, the case for the reliability of the Bible, and the truth claims of the Christian worldview for *months* before trusting Christ as my Savior. By the time I was leading students, I understood the role this information would play in *their* training. I knew these truths were the tools my students would need to survive in a hostile culture. But I also knew my students would need to know how to engage the culture with these truths if they were going to be effective. I needed to give them great tools and show them how to use them.

I applied the same approach my FTOs took with me as a new officer. Training officers are tough and brutally honest. They often told me, "The more you sweat in here, the less you'll bleed out there." They didn't hesitate to show me everything I might encounter in the field, and they readily critiqued my response. I take a similar approach when training myself and others to be Christian case makers. I do my best to prepare myself and those I train by engaging challenges from aggressive opponents. It isn't enough to understand the evidence supporting *our* side of the argument; we need to address the claims of the opposition directly. This requires us to examine the most hostile atheistic claims we can find. When I became a youth pastor, I introduced this approach to my students. I wanted them to understand what skeptics and atheists were saying. I was determined to *inoculate* my students, rather than *isolate* them.

If You Isolate   They'll Be   If You Inoculate   They'll Be
Them At   Unprotected at   Them At   Protected at
Home   University   Home   University

Inoculations are created from the viruses doctors are trying to defeat. Physicians expose patients to a *dose* of the illness so their immune systems will develop the antibodies necessary when they encounter it more robustly in the future. As I began to help my students process the claims of the culture, I prepared an *inoculation* that exposed them to a *dose* of the secular worldview. I wanted my students to encounter the claims of nonbelievers like Bart Ehrman, Richard Dawkins, Sam Harris, Victor Stenger, Christopher Hitchens, Daniel Dennett, and

Peter Boghossian while they were still in *my* midst. I didn't want their first exposure to these men (and their ideas) to be while they were in a university setting, far from a Christian response.

While there may be a number of atheist authors writing *against* the Christian worldview, there are even more educated, articulate Christian case makers *defending* the claims of Christianity. The answers are available and easier to access than ever before (refer to the Rebuttal Notes section for a sample). Christianity is experiencing a renaissance of Christian case making, due, in part, to the growing hostility expressed by the culture. When I first began to investigate the claims of Christianity, there weren't many choices available to people who were interested in evidence. That's not the case today. Christian case makers have emerged from every corner of our culture. There are many accomplished Christian philosophers, scientists, investigators, and authors making the case for Christianity today. I've written two books to help you discover and learn the truth. *Cold-Case Christianity* and *God's Crime Scene* include lengthy bibliographies to help introduce you to reliable Christian case makers (along with the leading atheists) working in a variety of fields.

Once you've examined the objections to Christianity, take the time to investigate the

Forensic Faith Training:
ARM YOURSELF

When it comes to Christian case making, you don't have to possess a PhD to have a significant impact on your friends and family. Start by surrounding yourself with trustworthy investigators. (Review the list of respected authors and online ministries in the Evidence Locker section to select appropriate mentors.)

But good case makers are more than resource *collectors*, they're resource *consumers*. Carve out time, and start learning. You don't have to become an expert to be influential. In all my jury trials, the expert witnesses I call to the stand aren't the people who decide the case. Jurors get to evaluate and discuss the evidence, and these "regular" citizens aren't typically trained in any specialty. Don't be intimidated by the challenge. You don't have to be a professional Christian apologist to be an effective Christian case maker. Familiarize yourself with the evidence and begin collecting your own library of expert witnesses. Jurors are allowed to ask for "read-back" from the expert testimony they heard during the trial, and you're allowed to refer to your own collection of experts if you've forgotten something important.

truth. Seekers and believers who want to hear the case from a Christian perspective have lots of choices today, and most of them are free. I've been writing at ColdCaseChristianity.com for many years, and every article, video, and audio podcast is free to download. There are many other reliable resources on the Internet; a simple search for "Christian apologetics" will reveal thousands of pages. Never before in the history of Christianity has it been easier to investigate the truth.

When was the last time you heard what the opposition had to say? Have you been isolating yourself from opposing worldviews in an effort to live comfortably as a Christian? You're not doing yourself any favors. It's time to get *inoculated*. Don't avoid the books, videos, or podcasts created by nonbelievers. Read what they have to say. Let their claims shake you to the core, if need be, and then begin to investigate their claims with urgency and passion. Remember, the authors of Scripture have invited us to critically examine what they've written, using our God-given ability to reason, test, and discern. God's not afraid of your doubts. He's raised an army of case makers to help you sort out the truth, and He's called you to be part of that growing team. You'll never be able to defend what you believe or help young believers if you haven't armed yourself with the truth. Get busy; time is short.

FORENSIC FAITH STEP #4:
INVOLVE YOURSELF AND HIT THE STREETS

Police officers deploy into "the field" every day. We proactively deploy into our respective cities, looking for trouble *before* it happens. We get *involved*. This is the one characteristic of our work that most dictates our need for training. We train in defensive tactics, for example, because we know we'll eventually be *involved* in a fight. When officers gather to train, we spend the first part of the session at the chalkboard, diagramming and illustrating the maneuvers and tactics critical to our survival. But at some point during the session, we get down on the mat with guys who really know how to wrestle. In this *hands-on* portion of the training, we find out who's been paying attention and who hasn't. Because we all know we're eventually going to have to wrestle, we take the chalkboard sessions seriously. We know we're going to face real challenges on the street; these difficult tests are looming on our calendar whether we like it or not. The pending challenges turn *teaching* into *training*.

In a similar way, if you want to embrace a training model in your own life as a Christian, the most important *first move* you can make is with a *calendar*. When leaders and pastors ask me how they can change the nature of their churches and youth groups, I tell them it all comes down to this: If you want to train more effectively, your *calendar* is more important than your study notes. You can increase your personal growth as a Christian (and any ministry in your church) overnight by simply *calendaring* the hands-on events designed to turn *teaching* into *training*.

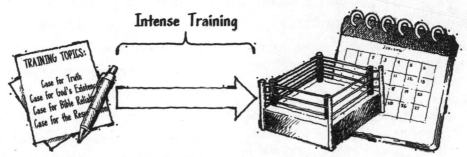

Intense Training

A Calendared Challenge Turns Teaching Into Training

Once I realized my calendar had the power to transform my Christian walk in this way, I began to schedule my own opportunities. I joined with others in street evangelism and service projects that stretched my knowledge and tested my character. I knew, in advance of these events, that I would have to prepare myself. The calendared events provided me with the incentive I needed to get off the couch and get to work. My calendar changed, and so did my trajectory as a Christian.

When I became a youth pastor, I immediately looked at the calendar I inherited. It was filled with the kinds of activities we've come to expect from youth ministries across the country. There were pizza parties and game nights, surf camps and lock-ins, snowboarding trips and wakeboarding events. I went along for a year until I lost that first class of seniors. I knew my calendar was part of the reason these young ex-Christians were no longer part of the church. So I changed everything.

I began to partner with Brett Kunkle from Stand to Reason (www.str.org). Brett is a professional Christian case maker, and he was once a youth pastor in Colorado. I hired him to lead my youth group on an evangelism trip to Salt Lake City, and after observing the impact the trip had on my students, I asked him to design a special missions trip to the University of California at Berkeley. Our goal was simple: develop two trips designed to turn *teaching* into *training*. Brett exceeded my expectations.[10] We began calendaring a week in Utah and a week in Berkeley *every* year. These two trips required all of us to step onto the battlefield of ideas as we dialogued with Mormons on the streets of Salt Lake City and with atheists in the San Francisco Bay Area.

Forensic Faith Training:
INVOLVE YOURSELF

You may not be able to join a missions trip to Berkeley or Utah, but you can calendar your own challenges:

1. Think of a friend, family member, or coworker with whom you've been wanting to share the truth of Christianity. Now set a "deadline" for yourself so you'll use the time prior to the conversation to prepare your case.

2. Take an afternoon excursion to a shopping center, public plaza, or college campus to conduct informal surveys designed to start spiritual conversations (see the Evidence Locker section for an example of a spiritual survey).

3. Start teaching a Christian evidence class at your church, or volunteer to teach an evidence series at a youth group or small group.

4. Establish a recurring Family Evidence Evening and use this repeating opportunity to demonstrate the evidential nature of Christianity.

5. Start an online Christian evidence discussion group. You can utilize available social media platforms or build your own blog on a simple blogging software platform.

6. Start a lunchtime Christian evidence meeting at your school or workplace.

Think outside the box. Be creative. Activate your studies by calendaring regular opportunities to put your knowledge into practice. Turn your learning into training.

The first trip taught us orthodox Christian *theology*. Mormonism has co-opted the language of Christianity but has redefined each term. In order to speak to Latter-Day Saints believers, we had to learn how to defend classic Christian claims about the triune nature of God, the eternal deity of Jesus, the nature of grace, the role of "works" and faith, and the truth about heaven and hell. Mormons reject Christian orthodoxy in these areas, and they are typically well prepared to defend what they believe. To prepare for this trip, we role-played and spent eight weeks training prior to traveling to Salt Lake City. Once we got there, we placed ourselves in a variety of difficult evangelism scenarios. We shared our faith and engaged Mormon believers at the temple in Salt Lake City, on the campus of Brigham Young University, door to door in neighborhoods in the city of Provo, and at a festival in the city of Manti.

Our Berkeley missions trip taught us to think carefully about philosophy, science, and the evidence for Christianity. Like the Utah trip, we began by role-playing and then trained for eight weeks prior to traveling to the Bay Area. Once we got there, we met with atheist student groups on the campus of the University of California at Berkeley, discussing a variety of important eviden-tial and cultural issues related to atheism and the Christian worldview. We also invited local leading atheist thinkers and authors to present their case. These sessions were followed by a question-and-answer period. Every Berkeley trip also involved several days sharing the gospel on the campus of the university.

We took the training for these trips *seriously*. Our trip preparation occupied *sixteen weeks* of our calendar every year. That's a serious commitment to training, and it usually *wasn't enough*. These trips were daunting and difficult. We came back to our lodging each night eager to study. We were usually frustrated by our own limitations and our inability to effectively communicate what we believed, in spite of all the training we had done prior to the trip. Every night we debriefed our experience, then allowed ourselves some "free time." Even though we could have used this time to relax, play games, or just get some sleep, we usually didn't choose to do any of those things. Instead, we stayed up all night *cramming*. In all the time I've been a Christian, I've never experienced such an engaging, intense, or purposeful time as I did on those trips. When we finally got home, we were exhausted but equipped.

These battlefields brought the educational experience to *life*. We learned what it meant to "be prepared to give an answer to everyone who ask[ed us] to give the reason for the hope that [we had]," and we did it "with gentleness and respect, keeping a clear conscience, so that those who [spoke] maliciously against [our] good behavior in Christ may be ashamed of their slan-der." We were trained to understand *why* we believed *what* we believed, and we came to truly love the people of Utah and the students at Berkeley. These difficult, taxing, labor-intensive opportunities turned *teaching* into *training*.

FORENSIC FAITH STEP #5:

NURTURE OTHERS BY DEMONSTRATING THE NATURE OF JESUS

I'll admit that, as a new Christian case maker, I often focused on the first part of Peter's biblical command rather than the second. It's sometimes easier to "give the reason for the hope [I] have" than it is to do it with "gentleness and respect," especially when the opposition can be harsh and unloving. I'm actually embarrassed of some of my behavior on our first trips to Utah and Berkeley. I was a protective "papa bear" youth pastor, and I often reacted harshly to atheist presenters who mocked or lied to us. I was probably less than Christlike in these settings.

Peter understood the relationship between evidential confidence and Christian character when he combined these aspects of Christian case making in 1 Peter 3:15–16. Our mastery of the "reasons" we have for our "hope in Jesus" should *result* in an attitude of "gentleness and respect." The more we prepare ourselves for battle, the calmer and more poised we will be in the height (and heat) of the struggle. The more "ready" we are, the more "gentle" and "respect-ful" we will be. If we hope to properly train ourselves to become good Christian case makers, we're going to have to develop the evidential *confidence* of Jesus so we can display the assured *character* of Jesus. His *nature* will guide us as we *nurture* those with whom we serve.

One thing is certain: there will be times when our interactions with the unbelieving world around us will require us to nurture and care for those who are injured on the battlefield of ideas. When we got the opportunity to engage non-Christians in Utah and Berkeley, we began to appreciate what was waiting for every young Christian outside the safe, protective environment of our church family. We often encountered smart, informed nonbelievers who challenged our ideas and beliefs. Sometimes these challengers were aggressive (and even hostile). When that happened, we began to understand our role as nurturers and modelers.

As a new officer, I participated in the California Police Olympics for three years. One of the most popular sports at the games was boxing. If you've ever watched a boxing match, you know how important trainers and "cut-men" are in each fighter's corner. Jacob "Stitch" Duran is a well-known cut-man who has worked in the corner of many famous boxers and mixed martial arts fighters. His job is simple. When a fighter returns to the corner at the end of a round, bleeding from an injury suffered in the past several minutes, it's Duran's job to stop the bleeding and get the fighter back in the fight. There are times when we also need to be "cut-men" for Christians who have been injured in the battlefield of ideas. Duran is effective because he knows how to address critical concerns quickly and return the fighter to the ring. As Christian case makers, we also need to be able to address the critical concerns of our Christian family members so we can overcome the "injuries" we may suffer in our ever more hostile culture.

Duran wouldn't be of much use to his fighters, however, if he lacked the right tools and training. Your effectiveness as a good, nurturing "cut-man" is similarly dependent on your tools and training. You don't have to have all the possible answers or be an expert to respond effectively. If you can simply *start* to make the case and know where to find the additional answers you'll need to help others, you'll be able to nurture people through their questions and concerns. As a parent and youth pastor, I didn't always have all the answers, but I was familiar enough with each issue and objection to nurture my students through a crisis. Our youth ministry team faced one such crisis on our first missions trip to UC Berkeley.

We took a student, Jenna, with us on this trip. Jenna wasn't a regular member of our group. She joined us late in the training process and missed the first two training sessions. Being new, she didn't have close relationships with many of the students in our group. On the first night of our trip, we invited a local atheist to come in and present his case for atheism. He was particularly aggressive, and made the following statement:

Okay, students, I am going to describe an ancient deity and I want you to tell me who it is. The god I am thinking of was …

Born of a virgin, in a cave, on December 25

His birth was attended by shepherds

He was considered a great traveling teacher and master

He had twelve companions (or disciples) and promised his followers immortality

He performed miracles and sacrificed himself for world peace

He was buried in a tomb and after three days rose again

His followers celebrated this event each year at the time of his resurrection (and this date later became "Easter")

He was called the "Good Shepherd," was identified with both the Lamb and the Lion

He was considered to be the "Way, the Truth and the Light," the "Logos," the "Redeemer," the "Savior," and the "Messiah"

His followers celebrated Sunday as his sacred day (also known as the "Lord's Day")

His followers celebrated a Eucharist or "Lord's Supper"

So, students, who am I describing?

I was sitting in the back of the room, and I already knew where the speaker was trying to lead my students. Although most of them were prepared for his approach, Jenna was not.

"You're talking about Jesus," she said confidently.

"No, I'm not talking about Jesus at all," the speaker responded. "I'm talking about Mithras, an ancient Persian mythological figure who preceded Jesus by four hundred years. In fact, the story of Jesus is simply a borrowed piece of mythology, stolen from other similar myths. None of the story about Jesus is true; in fact, there is no evidence to support the claim that Jesus lived at all."

Jenna was visibly shaken. At that time, I wasn't an expert on Mithras, but I knew enough from my reading to know the speaker was wrong about his claims. The list of similarities he offered between Mithras and Jesus were fallacious, and I knew any limited resemblance between Mithraic followers and early Christians was actually due to the borrowing on the part of Mithraic followers *after* they were exposed to Christianity. In addition, there is significant historical and textual evidence to support the claims of the New Testament about Jesus (as I've described in *Cold-Case Christianity*). Although I knew the truth, Jenna was unaware of the facts.

Forensic Faith Training:
NURTURE OTHERS

Few church ministries are as short handed as *youth ministries*. For this reason, most youth pastors are eager to accept help from people who are willing to serve wherever needed. When I first started working with young Christians, I was simply asked to sit in with a Sunday school teacher to help in *any* way possible. I found that most of my time was spent *answering questions*. I learned how to nurture in that early classroom, and it never would have happened if I hadn't put myself in a place where young people needed a mentor.

Have you put yourself in a similar place? Who are you mentoring? Where are you helping and serving the needs of others? Opportunities abound if we will only look for them.

After the talk, Jenna approached me and was at the point of tears. "That was so disturbing. It really shook my confidence, if I am honest with you. I'm not even sure that I can pray tonight because now I'm not sure there's really a God to pray to." I'll never forget her words. We spent the next two hours as a team, debriefing our time with the atheist and examining the evidence related to his claims. I shared what I knew about

Mithras and turned to some of the texts and resources we brought on the trip to highlight the many factual errors our atheist guest had presented (since this trip, I've written extensively about Mithras at ColdCaseChristianity.com). As a team, we knew enough about the truth to act as Jenna's "cut-men." By the end of our trip, Jenna was more confident than she had ever been.

If you want to nurture those who are wounded by aggressive challengers, you'll need to be prepared *in advance*. Like "Stitch" Duran, you'll have to be ready *before* the battle, so you can be helpful *during* the battle. Duran comes to the fight prepared for the worst. He knows he can't "ramp up" and learn how to treat the injury once the fight has started; he needs to be ready beforehand. Are you ready? Do you know enough to at least get started? When a fellow believer comes to you with his or her first doubt, unanswered challenge, or skeptical question, are you prepared with an answer or a resource? Has your preparation helped you to develop the certainty and character of Jesus? Are you able to respond with gentleness and respect? All too often, we are unable to answer critical challenges or nurture ideological injuries. I do my best to be prepared, in advance, so I can equip and nurture my injured friends and family members.

Forensic Faith Challenge:

CHRISTIANS ARE HYPOCRITES

The hypocrisy of Christian believers is often cited by nonbelievers. One popular Internet meme declares, "I've got nothing against God; it's His fan club I can't stand." Author Brennan Manning once put it this way: "The greatest single cause of atheism in the world today is Christians: who acknowledge Jesus with their lips, walk out the door, and deny Him by their lifestyle. That is what an unbelieving world simply finds unbelievable."[11] How would you respond to this common objection?

For a suggested response and resources to help you answer similar objections, see the Rebuttal Notes section.

I know this sounds like a daunting task, but remember, you don't have to become an expert to nurture and lead others. If you're willing to improve your case-making abilities, you'll be far more prepared next year than you are today, and even the simplest step of preparation may be enough to make an impact on the people around you. Don't be intimidated. A little preparation is better than no preparation at all. Start now: train *yourself* so you can help *others*.

GOOD CHRISTIANS NEED TO BE GREAT TRAINERS

One Sunday after writing *Cold-Case Christianity*, I was speaking at a church in Southern California. At the book table following one of the services, a woman approached me and asked to buy a copy of my book. She asked me to sign it for her twenty-six-year-old son. She told me her son became an atheist in college and she was hoping my book would persuade him to reconsider. I felt bad for this woman, but I knew I needed to be honest with her.

"I'll be happy to sign a copy of my book for your son, but I bet he won't read it." The woman seemed surprised by my statement. "If he's already told you he's now an atheist, odds are good he won't even open my book. But let me ask you a question: Years ago, when he first came home from college on winter, spring, or summer break, did he give you some reason to believe he was starting to doubt Christianity?"

"Yes, he asked a few questions. I couldn't really answer them. I knew he was being challenged by some of his professors, but I wasn't sure what to tell him," she replied reluctantly.

Forensic Faith Assignment:

SET A TRAINING SCHEDULE

Every officer in the state of California must continue to train on a regular basis to be certified by the Commission on Peace Officer Standards and Training. Agencies accomplish this by calendaring regular training for their personnel. It's expensive and time consuming, but necessary. If you want to be a competent police officer, you need to train *regularly*.

Your personal calendar is filled with *something*, but is it filled with the *right* things? Now is the time to schedule some regular training. What day each week can you set aside time to study and read? What day each month will you dedicate to a practical application of what you've learned? Get your calendar. Change your life.

It was heartbreaking. "I completely understand, and I hear this from parents all over the country. When our kids start to express their doubts, we usually point them to a Christian 'apologetics' book for answers. That's not actually what they want, however. When our kids share their doubts, they need to hear what *we* have to say about their concerns. It turns out that the first Christian 'apologist' our children need to hear from is *us*."

I handed her a copy of my book and challenged her to accept her duty as a Christian case maker. I encouraged her to *begin training*, "I'll give you a copy of *Cold-Case Christianity*, but you have to promise me something. I don't want you to give this book to your son until *you've* first read it. Master the evidence I've described, then begin to talk to others about what you've learned. In fact, I want you to start to actively share your faith and plan interactions with nonbelievers. I know this sounds like a lot to ask, but if you do this, the next time you get a chance to talk to your son, you'll be ready to answer him in a loving way, given what you know about him as your son. Is your son worth this kind of effort? You know he is."

Now, more than ever, parents need to raise their children with a *forensic faith*. We need to be ready to answer their questions and raise them with the evidential confidence they will need to stand tall in the midst of the pressure they will inevitably experience in the university. Training matters.

"MUSCLE MEMORY" AND CHRISTIAN CASE MAKING

Police officers understand the importance of training. In fact, training opportunities are regularly scheduled into our deployment calendar. We train every month, especially when it comes to the use of our weapons. Officers are required to visit the pistol range on a regular basis so we can qualify with our handguns and rifles. Our range masters take these opportunities to run drills in an effort to ingrain important principles. One of these exercises is known as a "failure drill." The range master inserts a plastic "dummy round" into our handguns in a position within the magazine that is unknown to each shooter. As we begin to shoot through the exercise, each of us will eventually engage the dummy round. This plastic round will cause the weapon to misfire or jam. It's at this moment that each shooter must employ a series of steps in order to clear the jammed dummy round. As officers, we're familiar with the required steps because we've been doing this drill for many years. Repetition pays an important dividend. When our weapons fail, our prior training helps us to reflexively clear the jam and assess the weapon. In fact, we don't even need to think about what we are doing anymore; these steps have become a part of our "muscle memory."

When you repeatedly perform the same physical process over and over again, your actions become a matter of muscular "habit." Your body almost seems to be working on its own, responding from muscle memory rather than reacting to mental commands. Muscle memory is important to police officers, because real gun battles are unpredictable and often involve an ammunition jam. The last thing you want in a situation like this is the mental distraction of a weapon failure. If you can relegate the resolution of this failure to muscle memory (rather than mental effort), you're far more likely to succeed. That's why we repeatedly conduct failure drills. These drills reveal an important principle:

> When the pressure is on, we resort to our training.

Read that again. It's an important truth. In stressful situations, it all comes down to muscle memory, and muscle memory is a product of repetitive training.

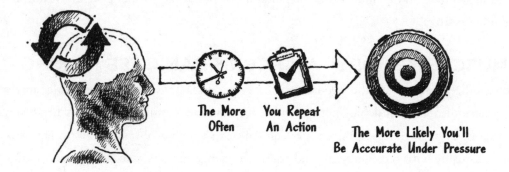

The More Often You Repeat An Action
The More Likely You'll Be Acccurate Under Pressure

That's why the best Christian case makers are the ones who continually engage the culture and respond to the challenges levied by unbelievers. The best case makers see each opportunity to engage others as an act of *training*, if nothing else. It doesn't matter how small the opportunity. You may be in a brief one-on-one conversation with a coworker, or you may be talking with a waiter about issues in the culture; whatever the situation, the more you engage, the more you train, the more your case-making efforts will become part of your muscle memory.

If you're eager to embrace a *forensic faith*, you'll need to start by embracing your *duty* as a Christian case maker and dedicating yourself to *training*. Once you've taken these two steps, you'll be ready to take the next: now it's time to develop the investigative habits of a detective.

Chapter Three

INTENSE INVESTIGATION

5 Practices to Help You Examine the Claims
of Christianity Like a Good Detective

"Here then, is the real problem of our negligence. We fail in our duty to study God's Word not so much because it is difficult to understand, not so much because it is dull and boring, but because it is work. Our problem is not a lack of intelligence or a lack of passion. Our problem is that we are lazy."[1]

R. C. Sproul

"Every Christian who does not study, really study, the Bible every day is a fool."

R. A. Torrey

"I'm not so sure you've got the right guy this time …"

Keith Morrison, the iconic television journalist and anchor of NBC's *Dateline*, leaned back in his chair. His right elbow was propped against his crossed left arm, and he was cradling his chin in his right hand. I'd seen this mischievous, questioning expression many times in the past several years as we chronicled a number of my cold cases. It was difficult to determine if Keith was speaking candidly or just testing me for the sake of the interview.

"Come on, Jim. What makes you so sure Mike's the killer?"

Michael Lubahn murdered his wife, Carol, in 1981, disposed of her body, and told the police she had run away from home. Carol was twenty-seven years old at the time, and she and Mike had two small children. Everyone believed Mike's story, including Carol's family and the detective who was originally assigned the missing-persons case. Over thirty years later, after a long cold-case investigation, we convicted Mike of Carol's murder, even though both families and nearly everyone who knew Mike didn't believe he was capable of the crime.

The case was incredibly difficult. There wasn't a single piece of physical evidence; our agency didn't begin working the case as a homicide until six years after the murder. We couldn't answer several key questions for the jury. How did Mike kill Carol? Where in the house did he commit the crime? How did he dispose of her body and move her car? How did he commit the murder (and the subsequent cover-up) without alerting his own children? In spite of these unanswered questions, the jury found Mike guilty after approximately four short hours of deliberation.

A week after the verdict, I found myself taping another episode of *Dateline*, but this time Keith was challenging my conclusions. He'd read the reports, and the *Dateline* film crew had been present during the trial. In spite of what the jury might have thought, there were just too many unanswered questions for Keith's liking.

"This case is just like all the other cases, Keith," I began. "It's not any *one* thing that demonstrates Mike's guilt; it's the collection of *everything* that demonstrates his guilt."

I soon realized I was more confident of Mike's involvement in the murder than anyone else in the room. The cameramen, sound technician, and producer seemed to agree with Keith. They were unknowingly evaluating the three forms of belief I described earlier; they were trying to determine if my conclusion about Mike was evidentially "blind," "unreasonable," or "forensic." After four hours of interviewing, I wasn't quite sure I had convinced them, but I was still confident in my conclusions about Mike. I had been investigating cold cases for many years by this point in my career, and I understood the nature of evidence and reasonable inferences. Even though there may have been unanswered questions, I had more than enough evidence to be certain Mike was guilty.

As it turned out, the skepticism in Keith's questioning was edited from the final version of the *Dateline* episode. Weeks after the taping and prior to the final edit, Mike Lubahn removed any doubt about his guilt. At his sentencing hearing, he confessed to the crime and told us where he buried Carol. My certainty about Mike's guilt was warranted, even though we didn't have all the answers when we convicted him.

THE RELATIONSHIP BETWEEN *CONFIDENCE* AND *DILIGENCE*

Evidential *confidence* is often the result of investigative *diligence*. I've learned to trust the investigative process when making reasonable inferences. I was confident of Mike's guilt because I did what I always do: I took the necessary, time-tested investigative steps to evaluate the case, collect the evidence, and come to a reasonable conclusion. I was far more familiar with my process than Keith or the other members of the *Dateline* team. Maybe that's why I was far more certain of Mike's guilt.

Our Christian confidence can be similarly bolstered if we apply a little investigative diligence to our daily lives as Christ followers. Once we've accepted our evidential *duty* and embraced a commitment to *training*, we need to learn how to *think* like detectives. My experience as a cold-case investigator may be helpful in this regard. My cases involve events that occurred in the distant past. None of these cases has ever benefited from DNA or other forensic evidence (that's often why they went cold in the first place). In many of these cases, the original eyewitnesses are no longer available to us because they died many years ago. Fortunately, their statements were chronicled by detectives at the time of the crime, but, in many instances, these detectives have *also* died and are similarly unavailable to us. So as I reopen each case, I have the difficult task of trying to determine what happened, even though I have reports in which both the original witnesses *and* report writers are long dead.

Sound familiar? The New Testament Gospels present a similar challenge. As Christians, we want to understand what happened in the distant past, even though we don't have any DNA or forensic evidence and even though we don't have access to the original eyewitnesses or gospel authors.

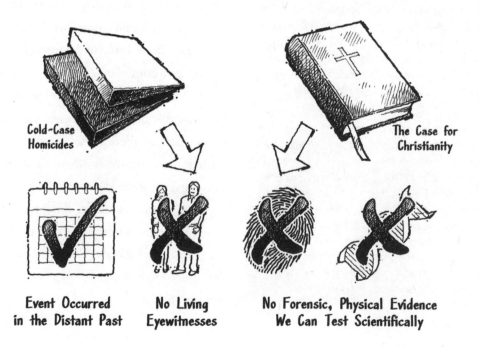

Cold-Case Homicides

The Case for Christianity

Event Occurred in the Distant Past

No Living Eyewitnesses

No Forensic, Physical Evidence We Can Test Scientifically

While this may sound daunting, the skills of a cold-case detective can make it easier. In *Cold-Case Christianity*, I shared ten investigative principles detectives use to evaluate eyewitnesses as I made the case for the reliability of the New Testament Gospels. In *God's Crime Scene*, I described eight investigative principles detectives use to examine crime scenes as I made a case for the existence of God. Here in *Forensic Faith*, I want to offer five investigative *practices* detectives adopt when examining (and solving) cold cases. These daily habits will help you transform *accidental belief* into *forensic faith*:

INVESTIGATIVE PRACTICE #1:
READ THE CASEBOOK COMPLETELY

Forensic Faith Definition:
PRACTICES

Police officers develop and employ particular "practices" in order to accomplish their goals. The term *practice*, when used in this way, refers to repeated customary or habitual activities or operations. "Actions" don't become "practices" unless they are done repeatedly or habitually.

If you want to develop a forensic faith, you'll need to start thinking like a detective and embrace the repeated *habits* detectives employ to investigate truth. When writing this section, I intentionally chose to use the term *practice* to help you see the importance of repeatedly rethinking the way you've been engaging your Christian worldview. It's not enough to simply read this book. You've got to start to put these concepts into *practice*.

In our agency, the cold cases are bound in red notebooks and stored in our "homicide vault." When I start an investigation, I pull the casebook and read it from cover to cover, including every original crime report, investigative summary, eyewitness interview transcript, autopsy report, and crime scene investigation report. Before I can begin a *new* investigation, I need to read and understand the casebook as though I were part of the *original* investigation. I'll confess there are times when it's difficult to stay engaged; some reports are more interesting than others. Some are downright *boring*. But if I want to understand why the original detectives failed to solve the case "back in the day," I need to be diligent and attentive "in the here and now."

I often rearrange the reports in the chronological order in which they were originally written. Old casebooks aren't necessarily organized in this way (reports are sometimes grouped by "type"), and some old casebooks are a *mess*. I reorder the reports so I can re-experience the case the way the original detective(s) first experienced it. Many of my foundational questions about a case are answered once I organize the reports in the correct chronological order. I then force myself to read the entire set of reports *repeatedly*, until I become the best expert on the case I can be. This requires me to be thoroughly familiar with each report; I need to know what each report contains and where the report is located in the larger notebook.

I've also learned to resist the temptation to read bits and pieces of the casebook *out of context*. It's easy, for example, to overprioritize a portion of a suspect's statement if you focus on *one line* from the original interview transcript. Statements that are taken out of context can make a suspect look guiltier (or more innocent) than he really is. I've learned the importance of reading through *everything*, from cover to cover, before returning to any one report, and I've learned to read the *entire* report before isolating any set of lines or paragraphs. It's all about context, context, context.

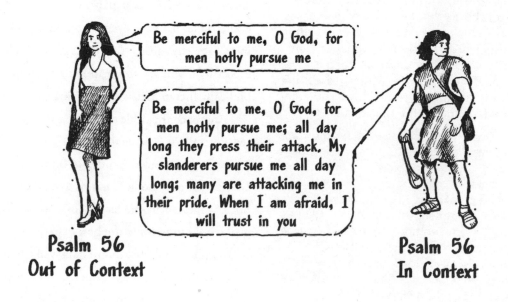

Psalm 56
Out of Context

> Be merciful to me, O God, for men hotly pursue me

> Be merciful to me, O God, for men hotly pursue me; all day long they press their attack. My slanderers pursue me all day long; many are attacking me in their pride. When I am afraid, I will trust in you

Psalm 56
In Context

FORENSIC FAITH PRACTICE #1:
READ THE BIBLE COMPLETELY

If you want to develop a *forensic faith*, you'll need to take a detective's approach to our Christian "casebook." I'm often surprised to find how many Christians still haven't read the *entire* New Testament, let alone the Old Testament. Don't feel bad; we've all promised ourselves we'd read through the Bible from cover to cover—and then stalled in Leviticus or Numbers. It doesn't take long to lose your "inertia." But while there might be times when it's difficult to stay engaged, it's important to push forward. If you want to understand the redemptive history of God's people "back in the day," you'll need to be diligent "in the here and now." Make a pact with yourself. Find a reliable translation you enjoy, and commit to reading our "casebook" in its entirety. There are a number of free Bible-reading plans available online to help you "stay the course," but if you just want to keep it simple, commit yourself to four chapters a day. At that pace, you'll finish the entire Bible in a year, even if you get busy and miss *sixty days* along the way. *That's* doable, especially if you are committed to becoming a biblically literate Christian case maker.

Approach the Bible the way I approach my red notebooks: read each "report" repeatedly, paying attention to the order of biblical texts. Learn what each book contains and where the book is located in the larger "casebook." The goal here is to become the best expert you can be, to understand the biblical data well enough to help others who have a question. One way to better understand the flow of history and

Forensic Faith
Investigative Guideline:
USE A COMMENTARY

Some of my cold cases are so old that the words used by witnesses in the original reports (their "slang" expressions and colloquialisms) are confusing. Unless jurors are familiar with the culture and conditions of the time, they'll have difficulty interpreting the testimony of these witnesses. In a similar way, biblical authors often use words (and refer to conditions) specific to their unique setting. Unless you become familiar with their culture and language, you'll have difficulty understanding the biblical text.

Don't be afraid to use a scholarly commentary as an aid to your Bible-reading plan. There are several good commentaries available on the market, and classic volumes (like Matthew Henry's 1706 Commentary and Adam Clarke's 1826 Commentary) are available online for *free*. These commentaries, when read alongside the biblical text, will help you understand what the authors of Scripture are trying to say.

the theological connections between biblical texts is to read the books of the Bible in *the order in which the events actually occurred.* Our current Bibles aren't organized in this way. Like my old casebooks, the texts of the Bible are often grouped by "type." After reading the text from cover to cover, take advantage of online Bible-reading plans[2] that organize the texts and daily readings in the *chronological order in which the events actually occurred.* You'll be amazed at how many of your foundational questions about the Bible will be answered once you organize and read the texts in the correct chronological order.

Resist reading bits and pieces of the Bible out of context. While it's popular to read passages of Scripture as though each verse was written for use in a fortune cookie, reading the Bible in that way often leads to misinterpretation. Biblical statements taken out of context can be incredibly misleading. My friend Greg Koukl has a clever saying: "Never read a Bible verse" (he's also got a great booklet by the same name[3]). Greg's not suggesting you shouldn't *read the Bible*, but that you shouldn't *read just one verse of the Bible in isolation.* Before you hang your hope on a biblical promise or build your case for a theological doctrine on a single Bible verse, make sure your interpretation is supported by the overarching framework of the passage. It's all about context, context, context.

 *INVESTIGATIVE PRACTICE #2:*
THINK ABOUT THE NATURE OF EVIDENCE BROADLY

My job as a cold-case detective is to find the evidence other investigators have missed, but if I limit my concept of "evidence" too narrowly, I may not see or read anything of evidential value. That's why I've learned to take a very broad approach when trying to determine what is "evidence" and what is not. Jurors are often unfamiliar with what qualifies as evidence when they are first impaneled, but it doesn't take long for them to broaden their understanding. *Everything* has the potential to be considered as evidence. In the many years I've been making criminal cases in the state of California, I've presented physical objects, statements, behaviors, and much more to make my case. Take a look at the variety of evidences typically presented in criminal jury trials:

Forensic physical evidence

Non-forensic physical evidence

Where the victim was attacked

Where the victim wasn't attacked

Items discovered at the crime scene

Items missing from the crime scene

Words the suspect said

Words the suspect failed to say

Something the suspect did

Something the suspect failed to do

I could go on and on, but are you starting to see the pattern? *Everything* has the potential to be part of an evidential case, depending on the nature of the case under consideration. Sometimes the simplest detail (something you might not typically think of as evidence) can make the case. I've successfully investigated cases prosecuted with nothing more than statements. These cases didn't possess a single piece of physical evidence, yet the juries came back with a guilty verdict. As I read through the original casebook of any cold case, I do my best to keep an open mind and examine *everything* for its potential evidential value.

FORENSIC FAITH PRACTICE #2:
THINK ABOUT THE EVIDENCE FOR GOD AND THE BIBLE BROADLY

When skeptics say the case for Christianity is weak because it can't be built with scientific, testable, physical, forensic evidence, they simply don't know how criminal cases are tried every day in America. *Everything* counts as evidence, including the behavior of the people who originally witnessed the life of Jesus, the testimony of those who listened to the statements of these witnesses, the touch-point corroborative evidence of archaeology, the internal confirmation of geography, politics, proper nouns (more on that in a minute), and the deficiency of alternative explanations. These forms of evidence (or something very similar) are used in criminal trials every day. Read the Christian "casebook" with an open mind and broaden your definition of "evidence."

Before we move on to the next principle, this is a good place to respond to a common objection. I regularly hear skeptics say, "*Extraordinary* claims require *extraordinary* evidence. 'God exists' is an extraordinary claim. You had better be able to produce extraordinary evidence to support such a claim." This is, based on my experience, untrue.

In 1981, there were approximately 24,159,000 people living in the state of California. That year, 3,143 people committed the crime of murder. Most people were law-abiding, peace-loving citizens; very few (only .01 percent of the population) were murderers. That's an *extraordinarily* low number if you think about it. One of these 1981 California murderers (representing only .000004 percent of the population) was Michael Lubahn, the man who killed his wife and claimed that she ran away from home. Michael was a beloved member of the victim's family, and they refused to believe he was responsible for her death. I can understand why they would feel this way.

Forensic Faith Investigative Guideline:
IDENTIFY "EVERYTHING"

In this section, I've listed some of the forms of evidence we commonly present in criminal trials. Without opening your Bible, imagine a similar list that could be assembled related to potential evidence in the Christian "casebook." If you were trying to make a case for the deity of Jesus, what kinds of evidence from the Gospels could you consider as evidentially important? Be as broad and creative as possible. In the next section, you can use this list to take another step in the investigation.

It was an extraordinary claim, really: Michael Lubahn, a gentle and friendly man, representing only .000004 percent of the entire population, without any history of violence and without any apparent motive, was accused of committing the worst possible crime. The victim's family repeatedly told me this was an extraordinary claim that they simply could not accept, and even after showing them the evidence I gathered prior to trial, they refused to believe it.

The jury trial lasted about a month. As is the norm with my cases, the evidence was entirely circumstantial; but this case was *particularly* extraordinary. There was no physical evidence, no body, and no crime scene. Of all my circumstantial cases, this one was definitely the most difficult and "thin." It was extraordinary on many levels: the unlikely nature of the crime in 1981, the unlikely nature of the suspect, and the unlikely nature of the evidence available to us.

After weeks of testimony and a jury conviction, the family was still unconvinced. This was an *extraordinary* charge after all; shouldn't there be some *extraordinary* evidence before we lock someone up for the rest of his life? Well, that's the nature of *all* homicide cases. Thankfully, they are extraordinary and rare. In spite of this reality, jurors draw reasonable conclusions from evidence that is both ordinary and unexceptional. As a result, I've learned that extraordinary claims don't actually require extraordinary evidence. When the ordinary evidence points to an extraordinary conclusion, jurors are within their right to make a reasonable decision. When Michael Lubahn ultimately confessed to this crime (yet another *extraordinary* event), he proved the jury made the right decision with nothing more than *ordinary* evidence.

The same people who require extraordinary evidence to demonstrate the existence of God generally fail to see the extraordinary nature of their *own* claims. Take, for example, atheistic claims about the nature of the universe. Did everything (all space, time, and matter) come into existence from nothing through some natural process involving the laws of physics? Did life emerge from non-life in a similar way? Can immaterial consciousness and true free agency emerge from an entirely physical and deterministic universe? Can the laws of physics provide adequate grounding for moral obligations? When atheistic naturalists form a case for such extraordinary claims, they do it with rather ordinary calculations and evidences. They assemble theories derived from this evidence and they expect all of us to embrace their case. I actually think that's a fair approach to the issue, but I also think it's fair to use *ordinary* evidence to come to an *extraordinary* conclusion about God's existence (I do this, for example, in *God's Crime Scene*).

As you read through the Christian "casebook," keep a very open mind about what might qualify as evidence. We can make a case for the reliability of the Bible, the historicity and deity of Jesus, and the existence of God from seemingly unimportant statements and facts. *Everything* counts as evidence, even the "ordinary" things you might be tempted to overlook.

 ## INVESTIGATIVE PRACTICE #3:
TAKE NOTES AND ANALYZE THE CASE THOROUGHLY

Before I begin reading the original cold-case notebook, I make a copy of it. I do this so I can highlight the pages of the copied book and write my own detailed notes in the margins. I generally use colored pens, correlating a particular set of issues to a specific color. This helps me to think through the case more clearly, and it reminds me of those areas needing clarification (or further investigation). It also provides me with a way to form my own summary of the important elements of the case. I then write outlines and summaries of the important details. These outlines will eventually become my finished reports when I file the case with the district attorney.

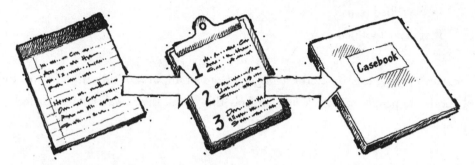

The Better Your Note-taking...   ...the Better Your Outlines..   ... and the Better Your Case

I try to be as meticulous as possible when citing and noting important aspects of the casebook reports, and much of what I consider to be important is a product of my training in Forensic Statement Analysis (FSA). I describe this discipline in greater detail in *Cold-Case Christianity*; FSA is an approach to examining the words used by witnesses and suspects in an effort to identify "deception indicators" and other important clues. If there's one thing about statement analysis you need to know, it's this: we all have a choice when selecting which words we'll use to describe something. Every time we choose a particular word, we are, by necessity, choosing *not* to use an alternative. This book (and every other book) is an excellent example of this process of word selection. I've tried to choose my words carefully in an effort to be both succinct and clear. You've probably done something similar, especially when deciding how to communicate with the people you love. The words we choose give us away; they often reveal our inner feelings, motives, and desires. *Every* word matters to detectives. My training in FSA guides the way I examine any report, even if it's something other than a witness or suspect statement. When I take notes in my cold-case notebooks, I pay special attention to a variety of textual characteristics, including the following:

Proper Nouns (Names) and Pronouns

The way an author, witness, or suspect describes someone is important. Did they use a proper noun? Do they ever change the way they identify the same person? If so, why? Consider the following options:

"Kathy lied to us."

"That girl lied to us."

"That crazy fool lied to us."

The words people use to describe *other people* are an important indication of how they see or feel about the people in their world, or how they think their *audience* sees or feels about these people.

Adjectives and Adverbs

Adjectives (describing nouns) and adverbs (describing verbs) are *optional*. Consider the following examples:

"Kathy lied to us."

"Kathy told us a malicious lie."

"Redheaded Kathy vindictively told us another malicious lie."

The reporter here had a choice in the adjective he used to describe Kathy and the adverb he chose to describe her telling of the lie. He could easily have simply *omitted* these adjectives and adverbs. His choice to *include* them may be an effort on his part to express his beliefs about her motive (she was being "malicious") or an effort to distinguish *this* Kathy from *another* (perhaps one who wasn't a redhead).

Contraction or Expansion of Time

How many words someone uses to describe a period of time may tell you something about the importance of the event in the mind of the reporter or may indicate an effort to conceal something. Consider the following three statements describing the same period of time:

"I ate pizza with Kathy."

"I drove to Kathy's from Pizza Hut. I took Hawthorne Boulevard. We ate breadsticks with our pizza."

"I drove to Kathy's from Pizza Hut. I decided to take Hawthorne. The roads were a bit slick from the rain. I don't typically take Hawthorne, but I figured the traffic would be heavy on Sepulveda. I was wrong. When I got to Carson Street, the light took forever to change. I could see the people in the car next to me were getting impatient. I thought for sure they might just blow through the red light. Eventually, it changed, and I drove to Kathy's. Oh yeah, I did stop at the corner to read my phone texts before I got there. I was late, but she loved the pizza."

In the first statement, the reporter failed to say anything about the drive to Kathy's house. If the reporter was typically brief in the way he described *every* period of time that day, this minimal description may not raise any suspicion. If, on the other hand, he included great detail in every *other* portion of the account except for the drive home, the *contraction* of time here might be an indication of deception, or simply a reflection of what he finds unimportant. The third statement includes a large amount of extraneous detail about the drive home; if this reporter was brief in the way he described *everything else* that day, his *expansion* of time may be an indication he was trying to conceal something *else* he was *really* doing, or may simply be a reflection of what he finds important.

Forensic Faith Definition:

FORENSIC STATEMENT ANALYSIS

Forensic Statement Analysis (FSA) describes a series of sequential techniques experts use to identify linguistic "signals" separating lies from truthful statements. FSA experts examine the statements of suspects and witnesses to identify indicators revealing subconscious information. FSA is an effective tool when employed by someone who has been trained in the discipline.

FSA is not a science, however, and we must be careful about our conclusions when examining statements. One thing is certain: the more we practice the techniques of FSA, the more reliable our conclusions. As you begin to look at statements more critically, be careful about jumping to a particular decision or inference. Cross-check and test your assertions and build a cumulative case to make sure your conclusions are reasonable.

While the contraction or expansion of information *may* or *may not* indicate something nefarious, it does, however, require us to examine the situation further. Does the reporter always compress or expand information? Is there another witness who can confirm any claims of the reporter? Has the reporter been caught lying about something else that would also cause us to doubt him here?

Apparent Illogical or Nonsensical Information

Witnesses, suspects, and report writers often raise as many questions as they answer, particularly if they are describing something they think is common knowledge or something they think has been previously described. Consider the following statements from four *different* witnesses:

> "They brought anchovy pizza to the party, even though everyone hates anchovies."
> "Because of Kathy, they brought anchovy pizza to the party."
> "Kathy lied and said everyone liked anchovies."
> "Kathy's obnoxious nature got them in trouble."

Each witness statement, when read in isolation, raises a question. When all the statements are assessed *together*, however, we begin to understand what happened at the party and *why* it happened. But the question remains: Why did each of these reporters leave out an important detail? The answer to that question may tell us something about what the reporter assumes is common knowledge, how the reporter prioritizes aspects of the event, or how the reporter really feels about the people involved.

As a result of my experience as a Forensic Statement Analyst, I find myself evaluating *every word* when I read a casebook. I wish I could say I limited this propensity to my professional work, but if I'm honest, I still find myself examining word choices when I sift through my daily emails, read news articles or blog posts, and even when I'm just engaged in casual conversations.

FORENSIC FAITH PRACTICE #3:
TAKE NOTES AND ANALYZE THE BIBLE THOROUGHLY

If you want to develop a *forensic faith*, you'll need to take a detective's approach to note taking. When I first became interested in the words of Jesus, I went to my local bookstore to buy a Bible. I'd never owned one before, but I knew what I was looking for. I wanted a Bible with large margins and lots of room on the title pages of each New Testament gospel and epistle. I didn't want a study Bible or anything fancy. I just wanted space to take notes because I knew my experience with FSA would dictate how I would read the text. My first Bible is nearly impossible to read these days, given the way I've filled every margin and every free unprinted space with colored notes. When I ran out of space, I cut new blank pages to match the size of the Bible and glued them in place with all my additional notes and observations.

I was meticulous when citing and noting important aspects of the New Testament accounts, and much of what I considered to be important was once again a product of my training. The authors of the New Testament chose their words *carefully*. Every time they did so, they were, by necessity, choosing *not* to use an alternative. *Every* word mattered to me as I read the New Testament texts. When I took notes in that first Bible, I paid special attention to the same textual characteristics I isolated in my professional work.

Now that I've explained some of the areas we consider when analyzing statements in criminal cases, let me show you a few biblical parallels:

Proper Nouns (Names) and Pronouns

How the biblical authors describe someone is important. Paul, for example, when writing to the Galatians, described his visits with Peter and James. Notice the way Paul described these men:

Galatians 1:18–19

Then three years later I went up to Jerusalem to become acquainted with **Cephas**, and stayed with him fifteen days. But I did not see any other of the apostles except **James**, the Lord's brother.

Paul called Peter by his Aramaic name, "Cephas," rather than "Simon," perhaps because Jesus referred to Peter in this way or because this region of Galatia was filled with Aramaic speakers. This choice of name may tell us something about the *audience* Paul was addressing. Paul also clarified which James he was talking about by adding the additional information "the Lord's brother." Once again, this may indicate Paul's audience was familiar with all the apostles, including James, the son of Zebedee. Just a few verses later, Paul again described these men (along with the apostle John), but chose to use different words:

> **Galatians 2:1–2**
> Then after an interval of fourteen years I went up again to Jerusalem with
> Barnabas, taking Titus along also. It was because of a revelation that I went
> up; and I submitted to **them** the gospel which I preach among the Gentiles,
> but I did so in private **to those who were of reputation**, for fear that I might
> be running, or had run, in vain.

Paul's choice of "them" may simply be due to the fact that he had already introduced Cephas and James in the prior lines of his letter, but Paul's choice of "those who were of reputation" (now including the apostle John, as seen in verse 9) is strikingly different and important. Paul could have said, "Cephas, James, and John," "Those who knew Jesus," or "The apostles." Instead, Paul called them "those who were of reputation." Why would Paul choose this expression? If we stopped reading right here, it would seem that Paul wants his readers to remember the important status and knowledge of Cephas, James, and John. Why? If a suspect did something like this in an interview, I would expect him to use the status of these men to support something the suspect said or did. Sure enough, this is what Paul had in mind:

> **Galatians 2:3–6**
> But not even Titus, who was with me, though he was a Greek, was compelled
> to be circumcised. But it was because of the false brethren secretly brought
> in, who had sneaked in to spy out our liberty which we have in Christ Jesus,
> in order to bring us into bondage. But we did not yield in subjection to them

for even an hour, so that the truth of the gospel would remain with you. But from **those who were of high reputation** (what they were makes no difference to me; God shows no partiality)—well, **those who were of reputation** contributed nothing to me.

Paul changed his term for Cephas, James, and John to highlight their status among the Galatians in order to legitimize Paul's theological position related to the gospel and circumcision. Paul told these authoritative apostles what he had been preaching to the Gentiles, and they affirmed Paul's position. They added nothing. Paul then used the status of these men *of high reputation* to appeal for the legitimacy of his own claims. Paul's words were an important indication of how both he and his *audience* saw and felt about the apostles.

Adjectives and Adverbs

In *Cold-Case Christianity*, I describe an important adjective used by Luke in the opening lines of his gospel. Luke actually uses a *number* of adjectives and adverbs in this passage (best seen in the English Standard Version of the text), and each one tells us something important about the noun or verb it is describing:

Luke 1:1–4 (ESV)

Inasmuch as many have undertaken to compile a narrative of the things that have been accomplished among us, just as those who from the beginning were eyewitnesses and ministers of the word have delivered them to us, it seemed good to me also, having followed all things **closely** for some

Forensic Faith
Investigative Guideline:

USE THE GAPS AND MARGINS

If you don't already own one, purchase a simple, inexpensive Bible with wide margins. Buy one you won't mind "defacing" with notes and observations. On your first review of the biblical text, feel free to note everything you discover. Include your rational and emotional impressions, reminders of things you want to research, and places where the text offers something puzzling or "troublesome."

On the second pass, focus on the four areas I've described in this section. After highlighting the words and passages, try to resolve any questions you may have on your own. For more difficult areas in the text, use some of the common resources available to examine challenging passages. (You can find a short list of these resources in the Evidence Locker section.)

time past, to write an **orderly** account for you, **most excellent** Theophilus,

that you may have certainty concerning the things you have been taught.

Luke appears to want us to appreciate the diligence with which he investigated the eyewitness accounts of those who knew Jesus. He could easily have omitted the word "closely" but chose instead to include it. When describing Theophilus, the man to whom he wrote both his gospel and the book of Acts, he decided to include the adjective/title "most excellent." Luke's use of this optional descriptor tells us something about the nature of Theophilus (or at least something about how Luke regarded this man) because this title is usually reserved for people possessing elevated rank or social status (Paul, for example, used this title when addressing Festus, the governor of Judea, in Acts 23:26).

There's one adjective that caught my eye when I first read this passage: "orderly." It wasn't enough for Luke to tell Theophilus he had written an "account"; he wanted Theophilus to know he had written an "orderly account." The Greek word used here for "orderly" (καθεξῆς) means "correct chronological order." In fact, the New American Standard version translates it as "in consecutive order." If Luke is writing a history of Jesus based on the eyewitness accounts available to him, why would he feel compelled to say his history is in the correct chronological order? Aren't *all* historical accounts in the correct chronological order?

Remember, additional descriptors are often used to distinguish one object or person from another. As we've already seen, Paul described James as "the Lord's brother" to distinguish him from other apostolic leaders named James. Was Luke's use of "orderly" intended to distinguish his gospel from another "narrative of the things that have been accomplished among us"? I think so. As I point out in *Cold-Case Christianity*, Papias, the ancient bishop of Hierapolis, described Mark's gospel narrative in the following way:

> Mark, having become the interpreter of Peter, wrote down accurately,
> **though not indeed in order**, whatsoever he remembered of the things
> said or done by Christ. For he neither heard the Lord nor followed him,
> but afterward, as I said, he followed Peter, who adapted his teaching to the
> needs of his hearers, but with no intention of giving a connected account
> of the Lord's discourses, so that Mark committed no error while he thus

wrote some things as he remembered them. For he was careful of one thing, not to omit any of the things which he had heard, and not to state any of them falsely.[4]

Given this description by Papias, Luke's use of the word "orderly" makes sense, particularly if he was aware of Mark's account and wanted to distinguish his own. As it turns out, Luke was clearly familiar with Mark's work, as he quoted Mark more than any other source (Luke used information found in approximately 350 of Mark's verses). Luke had a choice in the adjective he used to describe his own gospel, and by describing it as "orderly," he distinguished it from Mark's.

Contraction or Expansion of Time

Skeptics sometimes point to differences between the gospel accounts as evidence of their unreliability. When I first read through the Gospels as an atheist, however, the differences between accounts only strengthened my interest in them as eyewitness accounts. Why? Because witnesses *always* pick and choose between things they elect to report. Everyone compresses or expands time; the only question is whether this contraction or expansion is a sign of *deception*. Let's examine an example from the New Testament: the time involving the Sermon on the Mount. Matthew, when writing about this sermon, provided the following information:

Matthew 5:3–12

He [Jesus] opened His mouth and began to teach them, saying,
"Blessed are the poor in spirit, for theirs is the kingdom of heaven.
Blessed are those who mourn, for they shall be comforted.
Blessed are the gentle, for they shall inherit the earth.
Blessed are those who hunger and thirst for righteousness, for they shall be satisfied.
Blessed are the merciful, for they shall receive mercy.
Blessed are the pure in heart, for they shall see God.
Blessed are the peacemakers, for they shall be called sons of God.

Blessed are those who have been persecuted for the sake of righteousness, for theirs is the kingdom of heaven.

Blessed are you when people insult you and persecute you, and falsely say all kinds of evil against you because of Me. Rejoice and be glad, for your reward in heaven is great; for in the same way they persecuted the prophets who were before you."

Notice how Matthew provided a comprehensive list of "blessings" in his account. When Luke, however, described the sermon in his gospel, he shortened the list of blessings and added a list of "woes":

Luke 6:20–26

And turning His gaze toward His disciples, He began to say,

"Blessed are you who are poor, for yours is the kingdom of God.

Blessed are you who hunger now, for you shall be satisfied.

Blessed are you who weep now, for you shall laugh.

Blessed are you when men hate you, and ostracize you, and insult you, and scorn your name as evil, for the sake of the Son of Man. Be glad in that day and leap for joy, for behold, your reward is great in heaven. For in the same way their fathers used to treat the prophets.

But woe to you who are rich, for you are receiving your comfort in full.

Woe to you who are well-fed now, for you shall be hungry.

Woe to you who laugh now, for you shall mourn and weep.

Woe to you when all men speak well of you, for their fathers used to treat the false prophets in the same way."

Mark and John, when writing their own gospels, contracted time and omitted the sermon *altogether*. How are we to reconcile these accounts? Does the expansion or contraction of time and information here indicate someone is lying? Did the Sermon on the Mount really occur, and if so, why would Mark and John omit it entirely? While the contraction or expansion of information may or may not indicate something nefarious, it does, however, require us to examine the situation further. We can ask the same kinds of questions we ask in criminal investigations: Does the author *always* compress or expand information? Is there another witness who can confirm any of these claims? Has the author been caught lying about something else that would also cause us to doubt him here?

John and Mark's omission seems to be consistent with the nature of their gospels. Mark's gospel is remarkably brief *in general*. Mark typically said less than any other author and recorded events at a much faster pace (see more about the "crime broadcast" nature of Mark's gospel in *Cold-Case Christianity*). Mark may have omitted the Sermon on the Mount, but he was clearly aware of the information in the sermon; he repeated elements of Jesus's teaching throughout the remainder of his gospel (he quoted the Lord's Prayer, for example, in Mark 11:25). John was also generally selective in what he communicated, and even admitted "there are also many other things which Jesus did."[5] John clearly intended to tell his readers more about events that *weren't* covered by the other

Forensic Faith
Investigative Guideline:

INVEST IN YOUR INVESTIGATION

It's difficult to examine the importance of biblical *word selection* if you're not familiar with Greek or Hebrew. What was the original word used by the author? Did he use this word elsewhere? How was the word used by other authors at this point in history? As I began to study the biblical texts (and long before I completed my own graduate work in theological studies), I quickly realized I would have to better understand the biblical languages. I invested in several print resources and filled my bookshelves with encyclopedias, lexicons, and commentaries. I eventually purchased Bible study software.

If you want to take the next step in your development as a biblical Forensic Statement Analyst, invest in your investigation. Bible study software will put the world of scholarship at your fingertips. You can access many free Bible study tools online, and you can purchase excellent software to help you become a better investigator. Refer to the Evidence Locker section to see a list of Bible study resources.

three gospels (the vast majority of John's gospel is unique to John). Nothing in John or Mark's gospels would lead us to believe Matthew or Luke were *lying* about the sermon, and we have two additional accounts to verify the event.

Apparent Illogical or Nonsensical Information

Like eyewitnesses in my criminal trials, the gospel authors often raise as many questions as they answer. When we discover something apparently nonsensical, we owe it to ourselves to investigate the account. Here's an example from Matthew's account of the trial of Jesus. Matthew reported that Jesus was brought before Caiaphas and accused of blasphemy:

Matthew 26:65–68

Then the high priest tore his robes and said, "He has blasphemed! What further need do we have of witnesses? Behold, you have now heard the blasphemy; what do you think?" They answered, "He deserves death!" Then they spat in His face and beat Him with their fists; and others slapped Him, and said, "Prophesy to us, You Christ; who is the one who hit You?"

When read in its entirety, this chapter of Matthew's gospel presents us with unanswered questions related to Jesus's attackers. Matthew reported that the men at the trial challenged Jesus to prophesy about the identity of His assailants to prove His claim of deity. But how hard would it have been for Jesus to simply look at His attackers and answer this question? And why would the response to this simple query prove anything about the power of Jesus? Matthew's account fails to answer these questions. Luckily for us, Matthew's report is supplemented by another:

Luke 22:63–65

Now the men who were holding Jesus in custody were mocking Him and beating Him, and **they blindfolded Him** and were asking Him, saying, "Prophesy, who is the one who hit You?" And they were saying many other things against Him, blaspheming.

Luke answers the questions raised by Matthew. Jesus was *blindfolded* before He was attacked, and this is why His ability to answer the question posed by His attackers would have been evidence of His power. The Gospels possess many of the same characteristics seen in other reliable eyewitness accounts. While each account, read in isolation, may raise a question, when all the statements are assessed *together*, we begin to understand the totality of what occurred.

Don't be afraid to take some notes in your Bible; those margins are there for a reason. You may have been reading past some of the most important evidence in the Scripture. Now that you've seen some of the things that are important to me as a detective, I bet you'll start seeing them on every page of the New Testament.

INVESTIGATIVE PRACTICE #4:
SUMMARIZE AND ORGANIZE THE EVIDENCE USEFULLY

Detectives make lists. After reading through a casebook and noting important aspects of each report, I begin to organize and summarize the evidence I've discovered along the way. While investigating a cold case, I make *dozens* of lists, and these lists generally fall into two distinct categories: *evidences* and *explanations*. Cases are solved when one of the explanations on my list accounts for all the evidence on my *other* list. This process is called "abductive reasoning" and I demonstrate its value in both *Cold-Case Christianity* (chapter 2) and *God's Crime Scene* (chapter 5). My lists aren't arbitrary; they're *goal oriented* and *purposeful*. Consider the following example adapted from a case I described in *Cold-Case Christianity*.

A woman was bludgeoned to death in her home; the killer used some kind of large club. A witness saw a man wearing a mask, blue jeans, and work boots run from the location and drive away from the scene. The family suspected her boyfriend, and while investigating this man, detectives assembled the following list of evidences:

1. The boyfriend fit the description of the killer.
He was the same general height and weight.

2. The boyfriend lied about his alibi for the night of the murder.
When interviewed by detectives, he said he was drinking with friends. Detectives then interviewed his friends and learned they hadn't seen the boyfriend in weeks.

3. The boyfriend had an unexplained baseball bat in his closet.

Detectives served a search warrant and discovered a bat in the boyfriend's home closet. The bat was dinged and dented as though it had been used as a club, and it had also been soaked in bleach.

4. The boyfriend had an unexplained pair of blue jeans in his home.

The search warrant also uncovered a pair of blue jeans at the boyfriend's home, a pair that matched the pair described by the witness. The jeans were covered in dirt, but a luminol[6] test revealed an unknown detergent was used to spot-clean something (other than dirt) from the thigh and knee area of the pants.

Forensic Faith Definition:
CUMULATIVE CASE ARGUMENTS

Cumulative case arguments are typically built on a number of pieces of evidence, each of which may be imperfect or insufficient when considered in isolation. When examined in totality, however, the case becomes strong and reasonable.

Opponents of cumulative cases usually attack the imperfections or insufficiencies they observe in the single pieces of evidence within the larger case. But remember, each individual evidence is *admittedly* less than sufficient, and this has no impact on whether or not the final conclusion, given the overwhelming nature of the cumulative case, is reasonable. When evaluating objections to cumulative cases, help people to "see the forest for the trees." (More on this in *Cold-Case Christianity*, chapter 10.)

5. There was no sign of forced entry at the home of the victim.

Either the victim knew her killer and let him in or the killer had a key so he could let *himself* in. The boyfriend was one of only three people who had a key.

6. The boyfriend admitted to prior violence.

In a recorded interview, the boyfriend told detectives he commonly beat his girlfriend and often felt bad about it. He also admitted to beating her on the day of the murder because he found out she had been cheating on him. He even threatened in front of her friends to kill her but denied actually carrying out that threat.

7. The boyfriend owned boots like those seen by the witness.

The witness said the killer was wearing an unusual pair of boots. These boots had a vertical strip of leather on the side. After researching similar boots, detectives learned there was only one manufacturer of this kind of boot, and this brand was sold at just one store anywhere in the county. This particular store reported selling only thirty pairs of this boot in the past two years. The boyfriend happened to have one pair in his closet at the time of the search warrant.

8. The boyfriend was feeling suicidal.

When serving the search warrant, detectives also discovered an unfinished suicide note written by the boyfriend. In this note, the boyfriend said he was distraught over something he had done (on the day of the murder) and was so guilt ridden he wanted to kill himself. He admitted to losing his temper and doing something horrific, but he didn't explicitly say he murdered his girlfriend.

9. The boyfriend's car matched the suspect's vehicle.

The witness observed the suspect enter an unusual vehicle as he fled the scene. She described it as a canary yellow 1972–74 Volkswagen Karmann Ghia. When detectives searched the Department of Motor Vehicles database for this model of car, they discovered there were only a few of them still in existence in the entire state. With the search warrant, they discovered that the boyfriend had a yellow 1972 Karmann Ghia parked in his garage.

This list of evidence is useful because it organizes the data so it can be assessed and interpreted. This list makes a *case*. After reading these facts, the case against the boyfriend is clear. When detectives make lists such as these, we are, in essence, rehearsing our case prior to presenting it to the district attorney for filing consideration. If someone were ever to ask, "Why do you suspect the boyfriend?" this list would help me provide a response like this, by way of *summary*:

> I know the boyfriend is the killer because he fits the physical description offered by the witness and he lied about his alibi. He owned a bat similar to the one seen by the witness, and he suspiciously bleached this bat, probably to destroy any blood or tissue evidence. He also owned jeans matching those worn by the killer, and he effectively spot-cleaned something from these pants (most likely his girlfriend's blood). The boyfriend's boots were rare and also

matched those worn by the killer, and the boyfriend's car was an even more remarkable match. He was one of only a few people who could account for the fact there was no sign of forced entry, and he freely admitted to beating her and threatening to kill her. He even had a motive to kill her that day: he found out she was cheating on him.

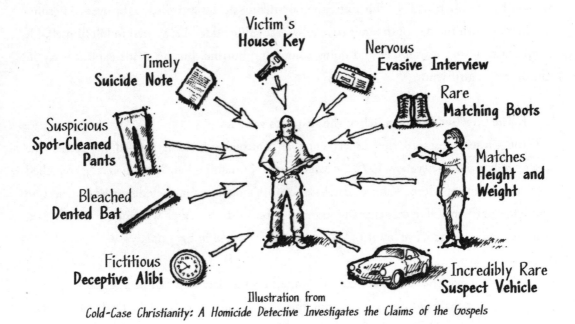

Illustration from
Cold-Case Christianity: A Homicide Detective Investigates the Claims of the Gospels

When I form evidence *lists*, it's much easier to form explanatory *summaries*. *Summaries* then help me make the case to others when they ask why I believe a particular suspect is the true killer.

FORENSIC FAITH PRACTICE #4:
SUMMARIZE AND ORGANIZE THE BIBLICAL EVIDENCE USEFULLY

When I first began to investigate the claims of Christianity, I heard many of my Christian friends say things about Jesus they had great difficulty supporting. On one occasion, I asked a simple question and offered a challenge: "Did Jesus ever really *say* He was God? I bet you can't find a single place in the entire Bible where Jesus said, 'I am God.' You know why? Because Jesus never claimed to be God." This challenge flummoxed more than one of my Christian coworkers.

When I finally became a believer, I decided to investigate the foundational claims of Christianity *evidentially* from an FSA perspective. I made lists citing some of the FSA characteristics I've already described. Here, for example, is a list of evidences demonstrating that Jesus *did*, in fact, claim to be God. To make it more memorable, I tried to describe each category with the letter *P*:

1. Jesus Made Statements about His Divine *"Place"* of Origin

When asked about His place of origin, Jesus repeatedly identified it as the same "place" where God the Father abides. While mere humans are described to come from this temporal world, Jesus said He and God the Father came from another kingdom entirely. When addressing the Jewish leadership, Jesus said this:

> **John 8:23–24**
>
> And he was saying to them, "You are from below, I am from above; you are of this world, **I am not of this world**. Therefore I said to you that you will die in your sins; for unless you believe that I am [the one I claim to be], you will die in your sins."

Later, when addressing Pontius Pilate's questions about Jesus's position as the "King" of the Jews, Jesus confirmed that He was *not* of human origin and that He and God the Father came from the *same* spiritual kingdom:

> **John 18:36–37**
>
> Jesus said, "My kingdom is not of this world. If it were, my servants would fight to prevent my arrest by the Jews. But now **my kingdom is from another place**." "You are a king, then!" said Pilate. Jesus answered, "You are right in saying I am a king. In fact, for this reason I was born, and for this I came into the

Forensic Faith
Investigative Guideline:

START MAKING LISTS

Start creating "evidence" and "explanation" lists. Begin by identifying some of the foundational claims of Christianity and start listing those places in the Bible where you find related evidence or explanations. Why do we believe God is all-knowing? Is Jesus a created being or the eternal God? Did Jesus demonstrate His deity in some way? What are God's attributes and how can we defend them from the pages of Scripture?

Examine the topics that intrigue or challenge you, or better yet, examine the issues your kids, friends, or coworkers have raised when discussing Christianity. Start collecting the evidence so you can make the case later. Keep these lists in or near your Bible (Bible covers are also a great place to store your notes). If you can, try to use some sort of acronym or other literary device (as I did with the letter *P* here in my list) to help you remember the list later when you make the case to someone else.

world, to testify to the truth. Everyone on the side of truth listens to me."

2. He Made Statements about His Divine *Position*

In addition to all of this, Jesus said many things that were nonsensical unless Jesus considered Himself to be equal *to* and of one essence *with* God. In Matthew 13:41, for example, Jesus said that both the angels and the kingdom were *His*:

Matthew 13:41 (ESV)
"The Son of man will send his angels, and they will gather out of his kingdom all causes of sin and all law-breakers."

In other places in the Gospels, the "angels of God" and the "kingdom of God" were described as belonging to God the Father, not Jesus:

Luke 12:8–9 (ESV)
"I tell you, everyone who acknowledges me before men, the Son of Man will also acknowledge before the **angels of God**, but the one who denies me before men will be denied before the **angels of God**."

To claim that *God's* angels were, in fact, *His* angels would be highly inappropriate unless Jesus and God are *both* part of the Godhead. Jesus also made a number of comments about His relationship with God the Father that would be difficult to understand if Jesus did not consider Himself equal in essence with God:

John 14:6–9

Jesus answered, "I am the way and the truth and the life. No one comes to the Father except through me. If you really knew me, you would know my Father as well. From now on, you do know him and have seen him." Philip said, "Lord, show us the Father and that will be enough for us." Jesus answered: "Don't you know me, Philip, even after I have been among you such a long time? **Anyone who has seen me has seen the Father.**

3. He Made Statements about His Divine *Parity*

Jesus made several statements that *implied* His deity, even before He made any direct statements *about* His deity. Jesus often prefaced His teaching in a way that separated Him from other prophets or important religious leaders. When Old Testament prophets made a proclamation, they would typically begin by saying, "Thus saith the Lord," or, "The word of the Lord came to me" (from the King James Version), or, "This is what the Lord says" (in modern translations):

Isaiah 10:24

Therefore, this is what the Lord, the LORD Almighty, says: "O my people who live in Zion, do not be afraid of the Assyrians, who beat you with a rod and lift up a club against you, as Egypt did."

Jeremiah 6:6

This is what the LORD Almighty says: "Cut down the trees and build siege ramps against Jerusalem. This city must be punished; it is filled with oppression.

Ezekiel 5:5

This is what the Sovereign LORD says: "This is Jerusalem, which I have set in the center of the nations, with countries all around her."

These prophets began their proclamations in this way because they were speaking *for* God, not *as* God. But this is never how Jesus spoke when making similar proclamations. Jesus typically began His proclamations with expressions such as, "Verily, verily, *I* say to you …"

(from the King James Bible) or "*I* tell you the truth ..." (in modern translations). Jesus didn't qualify His words to claim the authority of God as did the Old Testament prophets. Instead, Jesus spoke authoritatively in the first person using "I" as the only description for the source of His wisdom. The prophets spoke *for* God, but Jesus spoke *as* God:

Matthew 5:18

I tell you the truth, until heaven and earth disappear, not the smallest letter, not the least stroke of a pen, will by any means disappear from the Law until everything is accomplished.

Forensic Faith Investigative Guideline:

PRACTICE SUMMARIZING

My criminal arrest warrants are typically divided into three sections. In the first section, I simply describe the chronology of the investigation, recapping *what* was done *when*. In the second section, I provide a list of the evidences I believe point to the guilt of my suspect. In the final brief paragraph, I summarize the case based on the prior evidences I've described. While the first two sections are expansive, the third section is designed to be as brief and as powerful as possible.

That's the key to good *summaries*. Brevity and impact. As an exercise, read the gospel of John and make a list of all the evidence that demonstrates Jesus is, in fact, God. After making this expansive list, practice summarizing the list in a single paragraph of 150 words or less. Imagine this is the brief case you'll be making to an unbelieving friend. How can you recap the evidence in a short but powerful way?

Matthew 11:11

I tell you the truth: Among those born of women there has not risen anyone greater than John the Baptist; yet he who is least in the kingdom of heaven is greater than he.

Mark 11:23

I tell you the truth, if anyone says to this mountain, "Go, throw yourself into the sea," and does not doubt in his heart but believes that what he says will happen, it will be done for him.

4. He Made Statements about His Divine *Power*

Speaking again to nonbelievers, Jesus made the argument that His miracles alone should have been enough to demonstrate His deity. These miracles were proof that He was, in fact, God:

> **John 10:25–29**
>
> Jesus answered, "I did tell you, but you do not believe. **The miracles I do in my Father's name speak for me**, but you do not believe because you are not my sheep. My sheep listen to my voice; I know them, and they follow me. I give them eternal life, and they shall never perish; no one can snatch them out of my hand. My Father, who has given them to me, is greater than all; no one can snatch them out of my Father's hand. I and the Father are one."

The Jewish leaders knew what Jesus meant here; they knew that He claimed equality with God. That's why they sought to stone Him for blasphemy:

> **John 10:31–33**
>
> Again the Jews picked up stones to stone him, but Jesus said to them, "I have shown you many great miracles from the Father. For which of these do you stone me?" "We are not stoning you for any of these," replied the Jews, "but for blasphemy, because you, a mere man, **claim to be God**."

5. He Made Direct Statements about His Divine *Personhood*

Finally, Jesus made a direct statement about His identity as God, although it may appear hidden to those who don't understand the historical context of His words. When God first appeared to Moses in the burning bush, Moses was adept enough to ask God for His name. And God gave Moses an interesting reply:

> **Exodus 3:14**
>
> God said to Moses, "I am who I am. This is what you are to say to the Israelites: '**I AM** has sent me to you.'"

The Israelites revered the name of God ("I AM") as a precious title that was not to be slandered or given to anyone other than God Himself. Then along came Jesus. One day, when the Pharisees were questioning the power, authority, and teaching of Jesus, they actually accused Him of being demon possessed. Look at how Jesus responded:

John 8:49–58

"I am not possessed by a demon," said Jesus, "but I honor my Father and you dishonor me. I am not seeking glory for myself; but there is one who seeks it, and he is the judge. I tell you the truth, if anyone keeps my word, he will never see death." At this the Jews exclaimed, "Now we know that you are demon-possessed! Abraham died and so did the prophets, yet you say that if anyone keeps your word, he will never taste death. Are you greater than our father Abraham? He died, and so did the prophets. Who do you think you are?" Jesus replied, "If I glorify myself, my glory means nothing. My Father, whom you claim as your God, is the one who glorifies me. Though you do not know him, I know him. If I said I did not, I would be a liar like you, but I do know him and keep his word. Your father Abraham rejoiced at the thought of seeing my day; he saw it and was glad." "You are not yet fifty years old," the Jews said to him, "and you have seen Abraham!" "I tell you the truth," Jesus answered, "**before Abraham was born, I am**!"

Jesus made two remarkable statements. First, He claimed to be eternal and to have existed before Abraham. Just as importantly, Jesus picked a unique pronoun to identify Himself. He used the ancient title ascribed only to God: "I AM." The Pharisees knew exactly what Jesus meant by this. From their perspective, Jesus said specifically, "I am God." How do we know this was their interpretations of His words? We know it from their reaction. Once again, they responded by attempting to stone Jesus.

When I first started making lists like this one,[7] I glued them into my tattered, note-filled Bible. Like my homicide list, this list of evidences is useful because it makes a *case*. After reading these facts, it's clear that Jesus did, in fact, claim to be God. When, as Christians, we make lists such as these, we are, in essence, rehearsing our case prior to presenting it to others. If someone were ever to ask, "Did Jesus ever claim He was God?" this list would help me provide a response like this, by way of *summary*:

> Yes, Jesus definitely claimed to be God. He made statements about His divine place of origin, repeatedly telling His listeners that He was not of human origin and that He and God the Father came from the same spiritual kingdom. He made statements about His divine position as He claimed equality with God. He made statements revealing His divine parity, refusing to preface His proclamations the way Old Testament prophets did (with something like, "Thus sayeth the Lord") and saying instead, "I tell you the truth." Jesus also made statements reminding people of His divine power, offering His miracles as proof of His deity, and more importantly, He used the divine title of God Himself, calling Himself the great "I AM."

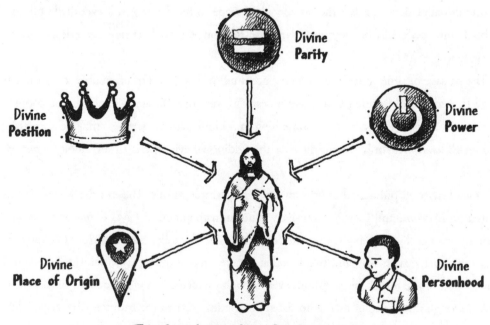

The Cumulative Case Demonstrating
Jesus Claimed to Be God

My *list* made it easier for me to form my *summary*, and a summary such as this is helpful when making the case to others. If my Christian coworkers had been *list-making* believers back when I was a questioning skeptic, they would have been ready for my objections and better able to make the case.

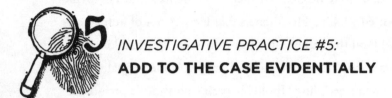

INVESTIGATIVE PRACTICE #5:
ADD TO THE CASE EVIDENTIALLY

There's a reason why my cold cases were originally unsolved: there simply wasn't enough evidence to "make the case" when the crime was first investigated. Even though some of the first detectives may have focused on a particular suspect, they couldn't assemble enough evidence to file the case with the district attorney. Although I begin the cold-case investigation by searching *inside* the casebook to find something these detectives might have missed, I know I'm eventually going to have to find additional evidence *outside* the notebook if I hope to file the case. I'll eventually fill another notebook with material from my secondary investigation as I conduct new interviews and collect new evidence.

The passage of time sometimes *helps* me accomplish this goal. I'm often able to use new technology to examine old evidence, and witnesses who were once hesitant may become cooperative over time. The suspect may even say something important over the years or may do something to give himself away. The only way to discover this additional evidence is to start looking *outside* the casebook.

One of my well-publicized cases is an excellent example of this. The murder was one of many featured on *Dateline*, and I wrote extensively about it in chapter 4 of *God's Crime Scene*. A woman in our city named Lynne Knight was murdered in 1979. The killer used a garrote (a strangulation device constructed with wire and two wooden handles) to commit the crime. The case went cold within a year of the initial investigation, even though the detectives were focused on one primary suspect, Douglas Bradford, a man who dated our victim prior to the murder. The suspect left the garrote at the scene of the crime, but the original detectives couldn't find any evidence to connect the weapon to Douglas. We reopened the case in 2003 and finally convicted Mr. Bradford in 2014.

The first investigators never conducted a search warrant, but I did many years later. We served the warrant at the home of Bradford's mother because he lived with her at the time of the crime. Amazingly, we recovered wire from the garage, and this very unusual form of *picture-hanging wire* was identical to the wire used in the construction of the garrote. Interestingly, Bradford's mother was a painter, and she kept a large roll of this wire for over three decades, using it to hang her artwork. Bradford evidently used the wire available to him.

In the time that passed between the murder and his arrest, Bradford formed a new relationship with another woman. This second female companion was willing to talk to me and described her conversations with Bradford over the years. These statements implicated him in the murder. In addition, this woman described how Bradford had stalked her in the past. We quickly recognized the similarity with our case: the suspect who killed our victim would have needed to stalk her prior to the murder in order to make sure she was alone. Bradford's more recent stalking behavior was strikingly similar.

By looking *outside* the casebook, we were able to collect several key pieces of evidence that strengthened the case against Douglas Bradford. When added to the evidence *inside* the casebook, we had enough to file the case and convict him.

FORENSIC FAITH PRACTICE #5:
ADD TO THE BIBLICAL CASE EVIDENTIALLY

As an ardent atheist, I scoffed at my Christian friends who continually made the case for what they believed about the Bible by limiting their arguments to verses *from* the Bible. "Okay, even if you think Jesus said he was God, based on verses from the Bible, why do you believe these verses in the first place? Why do you believe the Bible can be trusted at all? Do you trust the Bible just because the Bible says you can trust it?"

This form of reasoning was less than persuasive for me, and it continues to be less than persuasive for those who question the reliability of the Bible. When that happens, we need to apply this cold-case investigation principle by adding to the biblical case *evidentially*. The Bible is our Christian "casebook," and while there is plenty of good evidence *inside* the book, there will be times when the skeptics will demand more evidence, and they'll likely want additional evidence from *outside* the book.

As in my criminal cases, the passage of time can sometimes help us accomplish this goal. If you're making the case for the existence of Jesus or the reliability of the New Testament, the years have also been kind to your mission. Christian authors weren't the only people who wrote about Jesus. Over the years, many ancient authors added to the evidential case for Christianity. Once you start looking *outside* the Christian "casebook," you'll be amazed at what you find (I described a small portion of this evidence in *Cold-Case Christianity*):

Unfriendly "Pagan" Accounts from Outside the Christian "Casebook"

There are a number of ancient classical accounts of Jesus from non-Christian sources. These accounts are generally hostile to Christianity; some ancient authors denied the miraculous nature of Jesus and the events surrounding His life. But they also provided us with additional evidence *supporting* the claims of Christianity:

Thallus (ca. AD 5–60)

Thallus is perhaps the earliest secular writer to mention Jesus, and he is so ancient his writings don't even exist anymore. But another historian, Sextus Julius Africanus, writing around AD 221, quotes Thallus's attempt to explain away the darkness occurring at Jesus's crucifixion:

> On the whole world there pressed *a most fearful darkness*; and the *rocks were rent by an earthquake*, and many places in Judea and other districts were thrown down. This darkness Thallus, in the third book of his History, calls, as appears to me without reason, an eclipse of the sun.[8]

If more of Thallus's record could be found, we might find additional confirmation of Jesus's crucifixion. But there are some things we *can* conclude from this account: Jesus lived, He was crucified, and there was an earthquake and darkness at the point of His crucifixion.

Tacitus (ca. AD 56–117)

Cornelius Tacitus was a senator under Emperor Vespasian and was also proconsul of Asia. He is among the most trusted of historians. In his *Annals* (written in AD 116), he described Emperor Nero's effort to blame Christians for the great fire in Rome:

> Consequently, to get rid of the report, Nero fastened the guilt and inflicted the most exquisite tortures on a class hated for their abominations, *called Christians* by the populace. *Christus*, from whom the name had its origin, *suffered the extreme penalty during the reign of Tiberius at the hands of one of our procurators, Pontius Pilatus*, and a most mischievous superstition, thus checked for the moment, again broke out not only in Judaea, the first source of the evil, but even in Rome, where all things hideous and shameful from every part of the world find their centre and become popular.[9]

In this account, Tacitus confirms several historical elements of the biblical narrative: Jesus lived in Judea, was crucified under Pontius Pilate, and had followers who were persecuted for their faith in Christ.

Mara Bar-Serapion (ca. AD 70–?)

A Syrian philosopher named Mara Bar-Serapion wrote to his son and compared the life and persecution of Jesus with that of other famous philosophers. Mara Bar-Serapion referred to Jesus as the "wise king":

> What benefit did the Athenians obtain by putting Socrates to death? Famine and plague came upon them as judgment for their crime. Or, the people of Samos for burning Pythagoras? In one moment their country was covered with sand. Or *the Jews by murdering their wise king?* … After that *their kingdom was abolished.* God rightly avenged these men … *The wise king … lived on in the teachings he enacted.*[10]

This account adds to our understanding of Jesus: He was a wise and influential man who died for His beliefs. The Jewish leadership was somehow responsible for Jesus's death. Jesus's followers adopted His beliefs and lived their lives accordingly.

Phlegon (ca. AD 80–140)

Julius Africanus also mentioned a historian named Phlegon, who wrote a chronicle of history around AD 140. Like Thallus, Phlegon also described the darkness surrounding the crucifixion:

> Phlegon records that, in the time of Tiberius Caesar, at full moon, there was **a full eclipse of the sun** from the sixth to the ninth hour.[11]

Phlegon was also mentioned by Origen, an early church theologian and scholar born in Alexandria:

> Now Phlegon, in the thirteenth or fourteenth book, I think, of his Chronicles, not only ascribed to Jesus *a knowledge of future events* … but also testified that *the result corresponded to His predictions.*
>
> And with regard to the *eclipse in the time of Tiberius Caesar*, in whose reign *Jesus appears to have been crucified*, and the *great earthquakes which then took place* …
>
> Jesus, while alive, was of no assistance to himself, but that *he arose after death*, and *exhibited the marks of his punishment*, and showed how his *hands had been pierced by nails.*[12]

These accounts add even more to our understanding: Jesus had the ability to accurately predict the future, was crucified under the reign of Tiberius Caesar, and demonstrated His wounds after He was resurrected.

Pliny the Younger (ca. AD 61–113)

Early *Christians* were also described outside the Bible, and these descriptions provide us with more information about Jesus. Gaius Plinius Caecilius Secundus (Pliny the Younger) was a lawyer and imperial magistrate under Emperor Trajan. In a letter to the emperor, he described the lifestyles of early Christians:

> They had met regularly before dawn on a determined day, and sung antipho-nally a hymn to Christ *as if to a god*. They also *took an oath not for any crime*, but to keep from theft, robbery and adultery, not to break any promise, and not to withhold a deposit when reclaimed.[13]

This early description of the first Christians confirms several claims about the person of Jesus: the first Christians believed Jesus was God, and they believed He taught a high moral code.

Suetonius (ca. AD 69–140)

Suetonius (born Gaius Suetonius Tranquillus) was yet another Roman historian (he served under Emperor Hadrian). His writings about Christians describe their treatment under the Emperor Claudius (AD 41–54):

> He [Claudius] expelled the Jews from Rome, since they were always making disturbances because of the instigator Chrestus [Christ].[14]

From this account, we know Jesus had an immediate impact on His followers: they were committed to their belief Jesus was God and withstood the torment and punishment of the Roman Empire.

Forensic Faith
Investigative Guideline:
GROW YOUR LIBRARY

If you're going to start looking for evidence outside the Christian "casebook," you'll need to read some outside resources. Many of the historical accounts I'm describing in this section can be found online. Become familiar with the writing of ancient authors I've described in this section. If you can't afford to buy these resources and place them on your shelf, begin to bookmark the websites containing information related to these writers. Many of these websites are printable. When I first started my research (before I was able to purchase source documents), I printed a number of these sites and bound the materials in notebooks on my shelf for future reference and physical note taking.

Now is the time to grow your knowledge and your library at the same time. I've assembled some valuable resources in the Evidence Locker section to help you examine the evidence related to the historicity of Jesus, the reliability of the Bible, and the existence of God, all from sources outside the Bible.

Celsus (ca. AD ?–180)

Celsus was a Greek philosopher who was quite antagonistic to the claims of the Gospels, but in his criticism, he unwittingly affirmed and reinforced the very claims he sought to undermine. His arguments were quoted by the Early Church Father Origen. Celsus referenced nearly eighty different biblical quotes as he railed against Christianity, confirming their early appearance in history. In addition, he admitted the miracles of Jesus were generally believed in the early second century. The following excerpt is from Origen's defense against Celsus (the portions of the text that are derived from Celsus are italicized):

> He [Celsus] portrays the Jew having a conversation with Jesus himself, refuting him on many charges. First, *he [Jesus] fabricated the story of his birth from a virgin*; and he reproaches him because *he came from a Jewish village and from a poor country woman who made her living by spinning.* He says that *she was driven out by her husband, who was a carpenter by trade, when she was convicted of adultery.* Then he says that *after she had been driven out by her husband and while she was wandering disgracefully, she secretly bore Jesus.* He says that *because [Jesus] was poor he hired himself out as a laborer in Egypt, and there learned certain magical powers which the Egyptians are proud to have. He returned full of pride in these powers, and gave himself the title of God.*[15]

While Celsus was clearly hostile to the claims of the Christians, he provided yet more evidence of the Christian claims early in history: Jesus was reportedly born of a virgin, had an earthly father who was a carpenter, possessed "magical powers," and claimed to be God.

Unfriendly Jewish Accounts from Outside the Christian "Casebook"

In addition to classical "pagan" sources chronicling the life of Jesus and His followers, there are a number of ancient Jewish sources describing Jesus. These are written by Jewish theologians, historians, and leaders who were equally hostile to the Christian claims:

Josephus (ca. AD 37–101)

Titus Flavius Josephus was born just four years after the crucifixion. He was a consultant for Jewish rabbis at an early age, became a Galilean military commander by the age of sixteen, and was an eyewitness to much of what he recorded in the first century AD. Under the rule of Roman emperor Vespasian, Josephus was allowed to write a history of the Jews. He included the following passage related to Jesus:

> At this time there was a *wise man* who was called Jesus. His conduct was good, and [he] was *known to be virtuous*. And *many people from among the Jews and the other nations became his disciples. Pilate condemned him to be crucified* and to die. And those who had become *his disciples did not abandon his discipleship*. They reported that he had *appeared to them three days after his crucifixion* and that *he was alive*; accordingly, *he was perhaps the Messiah* concerning whom the prophets have recounted wonders.[16]

From this text, we can conclude the following: Jesus lived in Palestine. He was a wise, virtuous man and a teacher with many Jewish and non-Jewish disciples. He was condemned and crucified under Pontius Pilate. His followers reported seeing Him alive three days after the resurrection and believed this was confirmation of His status as the Messiah.

Jewish Talmud (AD 400–700)

While the earliest Talmudic writings of Jewish rabbis appear in the fifth century, the faithful rabbinic copying practices may have delivered reliable teachings from the early "Tannaitic" period (first century BC to the second century AD). Scholars believe there are a number of Talmudic writings referring to Jesus (many of these writings are said to use code words to describe Him). The following passage, however, refers to Jesus in a more direct way:

> It was taught: *On the day before the Passover they hanged Jesus*. A herald went before him for forty days (proclaiming), "He will be stoned, because *he practiced magic and enticed Israel to go astray*. Let anyone who knows

anything in his favor come forward and plead for him." But nothing was found in his favor, and they hanged him on the day before the Passover.[17]

From this single Talmudic passage (ignoring dozens more) we can conclude the following: Jesus had "magical powers," led many away from their Jewish beliefs, was tried for His actions and claims, and was executed on the day before the Passover.

Take another look at all the evidence for Jesus we've discovered *outside* the "casebook." The passage of time helped us to collect this additional data, just as it often does in my cold-case investigations. You may have noticed we employed the prior investigative principle here as well: we made a *list*. If someone were to ask you, "Why do you believe Jesus actually lived and that you can trust what the Bible says about him?" you could now respond by way of a *summary*:

If every Bible ever printed was destroyed and the only ancient documents we had mentioning Jesus were those written by hostile non-Christians, we'd still know the following: Jesus was a real man who lived in history. He was reportedly born of a virgin and had an earthly father who was a carpenter. He lived in Judea, in the region known as Palestine. He was wise and righteous. His teaching was so influential that He developed a large following of Jewish and Gentile disciples. He taught His disciples to live with the same virtue He exhibited, and His moral code was exceedingly high. But Jesus was more than a moral teacher: He possessed "magical powers" and had the ability to predict the future accurately. His supernatural acts and teachings persuaded many Jews to walk away from their beliefs. Jesus claimed to be God, and His disciples readily accepted this claim. The Jewish leadership ultimately brought charges against Jesus based on His actions and teachings. He was prosecuted and crucified under Pontius Pilate, during the reign of Tiberius Caesar. There was an earthquake and darkness at the point of the execution. Jesus's followers reported seeing Him resurrected three days after the crucifixion, however, and Jesus even showed them His wounds. His followers believed the resurrection proved Jesus was the Messiah. They adopted Jesus's moral teaching and lived their lives accordingly, holding to their belief in His deity, even though it meant they would suffer greatly at the hands of the Roman Empire. They were ultimately persecuted for their faith in Christ. That's a *lot* of information from ancient non-Christian sources, and it happens to agree with what the Bible says about Jesus.

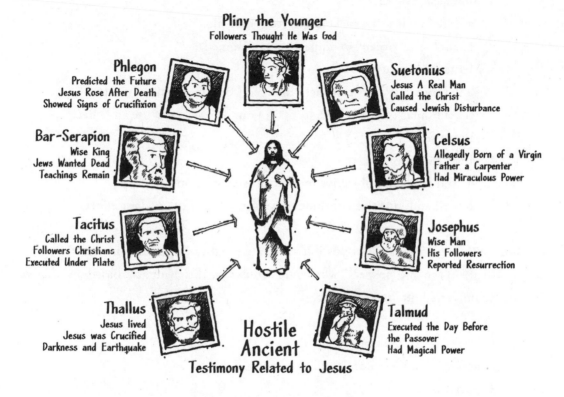

Pliny the Younger
Followers Thought He Was God

Phlegon
Predicted the Future
Jesus Rose After Death
Showed Signs of Crucifixion

Suetonius
Jesus A Real Man
Called the Christ
Caused Jewish Disturbance

Bar-Serapion
Wise King
Jews Wanted Dead
Teachings Remain

Celsus
Allegedly Born of a Virgin
Father a Carpenter
Had Miraculous Power

Tacitus
Called the Christ
Followers Christians
Executed Under Pilate

Josephus
Wise Man
His Followers
Reported Resurrection

Thallus
Jesus lived
Jesus was Crucified
Darkness and Earthquake

Hostile Ancient
Testimony Related to Jesus

Talmud
Executed the Day Before
the Passover
Had Magical Power

The case for the historicity of Jesus is strong. The record found *inside* the Christian "casebook" is a reliable account of Jesus's life and ministry, and it is strengthened by the passage of time as additional evidence emerged *outside* the book. There are many other time-assisted forms of evidence we could examine outside the Christian "casebook." In *Cold-Case Christianity*, I offer several examples, including evidence from archaeology. The evidence from additional sources *outside* the Bible strengthens the case made *inside* the Bible.

If you're making the case for God's existence, the passage of time will also assist your investigation. Current discoveries in science and philosophy only strengthen the case for God's existence. In *God's Crime Scene*, I offer eight pieces of evidence from four very distinct investigative categories, all of which are *outside* the biblical text:

1. Cosmological Evidence

    a. Our universe had a beginning.

    b. Our universe appears to be fine-tuned for human life.

2. Biological Evidence

    a. Life in our universe emerged from non-life.

    b. Biological organisms appear to be designed.

3. Mental Evidence

    a. Nonmaterial consciousness emerged from unconscious matter.

    b. As humans, we are "free agents" in our otherwise "cause and effect" universe.

4. Moral Evidence

    a. Transcendent, objective moral truths exist in our universe.

    b. Evil and injustice continue to persist, in spite of our best efforts.

From this evidence list, it is possible to create another important list describing the characteristics of the one "suspect" who could *account* for this evidence. Based on what we find in the universe, our "suspect" is …

1. "external" to the universe

2. non-spatial, a-temporal, and non-material

3. uncaused

4. powerful enough to create everything we see in the universe

5. specifically purposeful enough to produce a universe fine-tuned for life

6. intelligent and communicative

7. creative and resourceful

8. a conscious mind

9. free to choose (and create) personally

10. the personal source of moral truth and obligation

11. the standard for good by which we define evil

Once again, these *lists* can help you create a *summary*, and this summary can help you make the case for God's existence. If someone were to ask you, "Why do you believe God exists?" you could answer by saying something like this:

> The cosmological, biological, mental, and moral evidence in the universe points to a particular kind of suspect who possesses specific characteristics. The evidence is best explained by an "external" suspect who is clearly non-spatial, a-temporal, non-material, and uncaused. Our suspect is also powerful enough to create everything we see in the universe and purposeful enough to produce a universe fine-tuned for life. Our suspect is intelligent and communicative, creative and resourceful. As a conscious Mind, our suspect is the personal source of moral truth and obligation and the standard for goodness. Only one Being can be described in this way; only one suspect can reasonably explain the evidence in the universe. God is the best explanation, based on the evidence from science and philosophy, without any reference to the Bible. This description of God does, however, happen to match the description offered in Scripture.[18]

As before, the evidence *outside* the Christian "casebook" supports and confirms the evidence *inside* the "casebook." With each passing year, the scientific and philosophical evidence continues to grow and point to the existence of a divine creator. So don't be afraid to look outside the Bible as you examine its claims. Scripture refers to *two* kinds of divine revelation. The first is available to everyone: God's existence is obvious from the *general revelation* of nature:

Psalm 19:1–4
The heavens are telling of the glory of God; and their expanse is declaring the work of His hands. Day to day pours forth speech, and night to night reveals knowledge. There is no speech, nor are there words; their voice is not heard. Their line has gone out through all the earth, and their utterances to the end of the world.

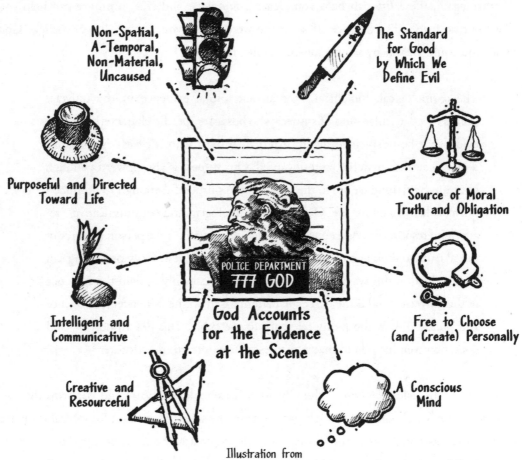

Non-Spatial, A-Temporal, Non-Material, Uncaused

The Standard for Good by Which We Define Evil

Purposeful and Directed Toward Life

Source of Moral Truth and Obligation

Intelligent and Communicative

Free to Choose (and Create) Personally

Creative and Resourceful

A Conscious Mind

God Accounts for the Evidence at the Scene

Illustration from
God's Crime Scene: A Cold-Case Detective Examines the Evidence or A Divinely Created Universe

Romans 1:18–20

For the wrath of God is revealed from heaven against all ungodliness and unrighteousness of men who suppress the truth in unrighteousness, because that which is known about God is evident within them; for God made it evident to them. For *since the creation of the world His invisible attributes, His eternal power and divine nature, have been clearly seen, being understood through what has been made, so that they are without excuse.*

The evidence we see outside the Christian "casebook," in the universe and in creation, is sufficient for anyone to conclude God exists. We are all "without excuse." But God has given us even more explicit (and specific) information and evidence. We have the *special revelation* of the Bible itself:

Forensic Faith
Investigative Guideline:
TEST YOUR KNOWLEDGE

As you read the answer I've provided to the question "Why do you believe God exists?" are you able to articulate the categories of evidence I've described? Can you make the case for God's existence from the cosmological, biological, mental, or moral evidence? If not, now is the time to better prepare yourself.

Get the resources (I've listed them in the Evidence Locker section), and pick just one area of interest as a starting point (the moral evidence, for example, is an area most of us think about every day, even if we aren't trying to associate moral truths with the existence of God). Start studying one category of evidence *outside* the Christian "casebook" so you can add to the biblical case.

> **2 Peter 1:20–21**
>
> But know this first of all, that no prophecy of Scripture is a matter of one's own interpretation, for no prophecy was ever made by an act of human will, but men *moved by the Holy Spirit spoke from God.*

> **2 Timothy 3:16–17**
>
> *All Scripture is inspired by God* and profitable for teaching, for reproof, for correction, for training in righteousness; so that the man of God may be adequate, equipped for every good work.

The *special revelation* of the Bible is *consistent with* and *confirmed by* the *natural revelation* of the world surrounding us. The case made from inside the Christian "casebook" is made even stronger by the evidence we find *outside* the book. The evidence we observe in nature (including the scientific evidence) is not opposed to the God described in special revelation. In fact, the evidence *points* to the existence of God (as I described in *God's Crime Scene*).

How God Reveals Himself to Us

Special Revelation

Natural Revelation

DOES ALL THIS EVIDENCE REALLY "SAY" ANYTHING?

At the jury trial of Douglas Bradford, both the prosecutor and defense attorney did their best to convince the jurors that the evidence "said" something about Bradford's guilt or innocence. This idea, that evidence "says" something, is a commonly repeated claim. I recently conducted a brief Internet search, for example, and discovered the following articles:

> "Health Benefits of Tea? Here's What the Evidence Says"
> "Making a Difference in Education: What the Evidence Says"
> "Is Print Advertising Dead? The Evidence Says No!"

In each of these stories, the authors wrote as though the evidence had something clear, emphatic, and unmistakable to *say*. Scientific facts are also often expressed in a similarly unwavering manner, as witnessed in the following online articles:

"ADHD in Adults: What the Science Says"

"The Business Cost of Climate Change: What the Science Says"

"Tumors and Cell Phone Use: What the Science Says"

These authors also wrote their stories as though there was little room for negotiation—as if the science has *spoken* definitively without any room for controversy. There is, however, a great deal of controversy related to many of these topics (just as there was disagreement between the attorneys in the Bradford case). Why? Because, as my good friend Frank Turek (author of *Stealing from God: Why Atheists Need God to Make Their Case*)[19] points out: "Science doesn't really 'say' anything; scientists do."

Scientific experiments provide us with *data*. Historical investigations (including criminal investigations) provide us with *facts*. The raw data and facts don't *speak*, *say*, or *tell* us *anything*. *Observers* and *thinkers* assess the data and facts, interpret them, and provide "findings" and "conclusions." The problem, of course, is that observers and thinkers

Forensic Faith Challenge:

SCIENCE AND RELIGION ARE INCOMPATIBLE

Ernst Haeckel, the famous German naturalist biologist, once wrote, "Where faith commences science ends."[20] Have you ever heard someone say something similar when they argue science is incompatible with your Christian beliefs? Have you ever been told, as a Christian, that your beliefs contradict what we know is true scientifically? How would you respond to this common objection about the relationship between Christianity and science? Can you think of two or three things you might say to someone who makes this kind of claim?

For a suggested response and resources to help you answer similar objections, see the Rebuttal Notes section.

(whether they are scientists, historians, or just common jurors like you and me) hold *presuppositions*, and these presuppositional biases affect the way they form conclusions.

If, for example, you are part of a post-enlightenment scientific community, committed to philosophical naturalism (the idea that nothing exists outside the natural realm of the material universe), you'll find a way to interpret every piece of data to confirm your naturalistic presuppositions, even if the best inference from evidence points to something

Forensic Faith Assignment:
ASSEMBLE YOUR INVESTIGATIVE "KIT"

As a detective, I learned to assemble a "call-out" bag so I would be ready when I was summoned to investigate a murder. My bag included (among other things) note-taking materials, a camera, audio recorder, flashlight, and latex gloves. My bag has become an essential part of my investigative experience.

If you want to develop a forensic faith, you'll need to become a good investigator. Start assembling an investigative "kit." My forensic faith kit is a small black bag (I used to call it my "truth bomb"). It contains my latest large-margin Bible, several colored pens for note taking, a number of colored adhesive "tabs" for book-marking, a small spiral notepad, a New Testament commentary, and any additional resource I may need to assist me with the topic I am investigating.

Assemble your own investigative kit so you're prepared to do more than skim the pages of the Bible. Your kit will help you dig deeper so you can make the case.

supernatural. If you are already committed to a particular answer before you investigate a question, you'll find a way to arrive at the answer you *started* with.

Let me give you an excellent example. Two young men (B1 and B2) were raised as Christians. Both attended youth groups and pursued their interest in the Bible in their college years. Both attended Christian undergraduate schools (B1 at Wheaton College and B2 at Lebanon Valley College) and earned degrees in biblical studies. Both eventually found their way to Princeton. B1 earned a master's degree in divinity; B2 earned a bachelor's *and* master's degree in theology. Both men continued their Princeton educations and eventually earned PhDs in biblical studies and ancient languages. Both married believing wives and became authorities on the Bible, examining the same ancient manuscripts and texts. Although both men have examined the same evidence, one is a devout Christian believer, while the other is not.

B1 is Bart Ehrman, the popular bestselling agnostic author of many skeptical books challenging the reliability of Scripture and the deity of Jesus. He presently heads the Bible Department at the University of North Carolina Chapel Hill, although he is a committed *nonbeliever*. His authoritative position has contributed to his considerable influence in our culture. Many nonbelievers point to Ehrman when making the case *against* Christianity.

B2 is Bruce Metzger, the iconic Bible scholar and longtime professor at Princeton Theological Seminary. Bruce's authority as a biblical scholar was unassailable. Before his death in 2007, he served on the boards of the American Bible Society and United Bible Societies, and was considered one of the best biblical scholars of his *generation*. Bruce was Bart's professor and mentor at Princeton; Bruce was the *master* when Bart was the *pupil*. Both men knew the evidence thoroughly, yet apparently didn't hear it "say" the same thing.

That's why it's so important to be familiar with the evidence itself, as well as what experts *say* about the evidence. I've never seen a jury trial where the expert witnesses got to vote on whether or not the defendant was guilty. Instead, *jurors* assessed the evidence (along with the experts themselves) and came to their own conclusion. As I described in *Cold-Case Christianity*, there are several reasons why people (even experts) might reject a truth claim, and not all of them are rational. Emotional and volitional objections are often powerful motivators, and these secondary impetuses are often the reason why someone rejects a claim.

Jesus understood this reality. When His disciples asked Him why He spoke in parables, Jesus cited the prophet Isaiah:

> **Matthew 13:13–15** (ESV)
> This is why I speak to them in parables, because seeing they do not see, and hearing they do not hear, nor do they understand. Indeed, in their case the prophecy of Isaiah is fulfilled that says:
> > "You will indeed hear but never understand,
> > and you will indeed see but never perceive."
> > For this people's heart has grown dull,
> > and with their ears they can barely hear,
> > and their eyes they have closed,
> > lest they should see with their eyes
> > and hear with their ears
> > and understand with their heart
> > and turn, and I would heal them.

Jesus knew that many of His hearers had a *heart problem* rather than a *head problem*. While the evidence was clear, their presuppositions and closed hearts wouldn't allow them to determine the truth.

So when someone attempts to discredit the Christian worldview or the case for God's existence by claiming the science or the evidence has already "spoken," remember: nothing could be further from the truth. The evidence and science haven't "said" anything; the *evaluators* have been doing all the talking. If these evaluators are committed to a philosophically *natural* worldview, it shouldn't surprise us they would find a way to interpret the evidence to meet their expectations and presuppositions. If you're careful about your own assumptions and biases, you'll be able to separate truth from error. I'm confident such an investigation will confirm the truth of theism and the validity of Christianity.

Chapter Four
CONVINCING COMMUNICATION
5 Principles to Help You Share What You Believe Like a Good Prosecutor

"His voice leads us not into timid discipleship but into bold witness."[1]
Charles F. Stanley

"There are four things that we ought to do with the Word of God—admit it as the Word of God, commit it to our hearts and minds, submit to it, and transmit it to the world."[2]
William Wilberforce

The prosecutor stepped up to the jury box and put his left hand on his waist, gesturing to the jury with his right and pointing back in my direction. He'd become very familiar with these jurors over the past six weeks. He learned about each juror from the questionnaires they provided prior to their selection, and he spent weeks studying their facial expressions as each attorney presented evidence. Now, as he prepared to offer his final remarks, the prosecutor drew upon an analogy.

"When Detective Wallace brings me a case, he has the difficult task of releasing it to me for the trial. All the effort he spent investigating and preparing the case for filing is complete. Now he has to hand the case over to *me* for the jury trial. I know it is difficult for him; it's hard for him to trust me with his hard work. In fact, I bet he still thinks he could have presented the case better than I did."

The jury laughed. They had been listening attentively for over a month, and I could tell they liked the prosecutor. By this point in the trial, they understood the work that was involved in investigating and presenting our case. They were also probably glad the trial was coming to a close.

"It's hard to trust your case to someone else. Detective Wallace did everything *he* could do, and then he had to trust *me* to do everything *I* could do. He did his job, and he hoped I would do mine. I know how difficult that was for him, because I am about to trust *you* the same way Detective Wallace trusted *me*. I've worked hard to *make the case*. I did all I could do. I did my job. Now it's time for *you* to do everything *you* can do. It's time for *you* to do *your* job."

I've been working with this particular prosecutor for over fifteen years, so I've heard him say this, or something like it, many times. It's still powerful for me every time I hear it. Why? Because it captures an important truth about the nature of persuasive communication. You can spend a great deal of time investigating, preparing, and communicating a truth claim, but in the end, you need to be comfortable *releasing* your argument. Do your job, rest your case, then trust your jury to do the right thing.

We've been involved in a few tough cases over the years. Some took longer in jury deliberation than we thought they would. As the hours and days passed without a verdict, we began to wonder if the jury doubted the strength of our case. At some point, however, one of us would say, "Remember: we did everything we could do. We did *our job*. Now it's up to the jury to do theirs."

That's good advice, even if you aren't presenting a murder case in the Criminal Courts Building in downtown Los Angeles. It's also good counsel for those of us who hope to present the case for Christianity to our friends and family. In fact, there are a number of things we, as Christians, can learn from professional case makers. The ability to communicate convincingly is the final characteristic of a forensic faith. If you want to be a good *Christian* case maker, consider the following five principles.

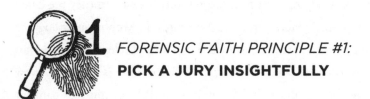

FORENSIC FAITH PRINCIPLE #1:
PICK A JURY INSIGHTFULLY

I'm often asked, "What's the most important aspect of a criminal trial? Is it the opening statement, the presentation of evidence, or the closing argument?" People are surprised to hear my answer. Most cases are won or lost well before the opening statements are made by prosecutors or defense attorneys. Cases are generally decided very early, at the point of *jury selection*.

Jury   Opening   Evidence   Closing   Jury
Selection   Statement   Presentation   Argument   Deliberation

You can have a great case but lose miserably if you don't have the right jury. That's why prosecutors and defense attorneys specialize in jury selection (or consult with jury experts who do). The procedure used to select jurors is known as *voir dire*. This Latin term is best translated as "to speak the truth," and it reflects the goal of identifying competent and capable jurors (from a larger "pool") by questioning them until they "speak the truth." Both sides search the jury pool to find impartial jurors who will view their case without undue bias. Potential jurors are questioned and, in more serious cases, asked to complete question-naires so the attorneys can learn as much as possible. Prosecutors and defense attorneys are allowed a limited number of "preemptory challenges" to exclude jurors they believe to be problematic. Once these challenges have been expended (or both sides are satisfied with the jurors they've selected), the panel is set. This process may take several days, and it's a critical part of the trial.

Jesus selected His twelve disciples, the group to whom He would make the case for three years, with care and precision, and all four authors of the Gospels captured this important selection process (see Matthew 4:18–22; Mark 1:16–20; Luke 5:1–11; and John 1:35–51). Jesus was intentional about His choices. Even though many people became His followers in the early days of His ministry, Jesus thoughtfully (and prayerfully) picked twelve competent and capable men from a larger "pool":

Luke 6:12–13

It was at this time that He went off to the mountain to pray, and He spent the whole night in prayer to God. And when day came, He called His disciples to Him and chose twelve of them, whom He also named as apostles.

Jesus was strategic and selective when choosing the twelve apostles. This group of men displayed many of the characteristics I've come to appreciate in good jurors, and as a Christian case maker, I've discovered the importance of recognizing these attributes in the people I hope to reach with the gospel. Before I make the case for Christianity, I think about "jury selection." Just as attorneys are careful to select the right *jurors*, we need to be careful to select the right *hearers*. Are the people we're talking to capable of examining the evidence fairly? Are they interested in hearing what we have to say? If we want to be effective Christian case makers, we need to be careful about who we select for our "jury."

When it comes to criminal trials, I've learned to look for three important characteristics in potential jurors. These are also important attributes for those we hope to reach with the truth of Christianity:

Good Jurors Are Passionate Jurors

Some potential jurors arrive for jury duty with great reluctance. They view jury service as an inconvenience and a burden. As a result, they appear disinterested and disgruntled. After spending years preparing the case for trial, the last thing I want at this critical juncture is a disinterested jury. Instead, I want twelve men and women who see their jury service as a *privilege* and *honor*. I want people on my panel who are excited to uncover the truth, glad to be there, and appreciative of their opportunity. Apathy is extremely dangerous on a jury panel. I'm looking for passionate jurors.

As a Christian case maker, I also recognize how devastating apathy can be. I didn't become a Christian until the age of thirty-five. I was an obstinate atheist prior to that, but after a careful investigation of the Gospels as eyewitness accounts, I changed both my mind and the trajectory of my life. As a new Christian, I was incredibly excited to share what I learned, but I wasn't always careful about picking my jury. Many of the people I engaged were uninterested in what I had to say. One good friend eventually told me I was wasting my time. "I don't give a rip, Jim. You're wasting your time with me. I'm not against what you believe—I just don't care." Now I don't honestly think my efforts were wasted on my friend. In fact, I pray and trust God will cause him to remember our conversations at some point in the future. But the experience only highlighted the importance of continuing to share the gospel with people who are interested in hearing what I have to say.

Jesus understood the importance of selecting passionate people who were interested in His message. Simon Peter, for example, was clearly a passionate hearer. Impulsive and energetic, Peter was quick to volunteer and eager to respond. He was also interested in what Jesus had to say. Peter and his brother, Andrew, had been disciples of John the Baptist (as described in John 1:35–42) and had been listening to John's teaching about the coming Messiah. One day, Andrew heard John identify Jesus as the Messiah, "the Lamb of God." Andrew found his brother, Simon, and the two men quickly became Jesus's disciples. Both were passionate and receptive.

As I travel, work, and play, I'm looking for signs of God's involvement in the lives of the nonbelievers I know. There are some people I've known for years who suddenly become passionately interested in the things of God; when I see that happen, I impanel them on my jury as fast as I can. God is already moving in their lives, and now it's time for me to make the case. I am only a small part of what God is doing, but I am ready to play my role, helping to remove the obstacles and answer the tough questions.

Good Jurors Are Unbiased Jurors

We ask jurors if they can be fair when making a decision, even though we know they have opinions and biases. As humans, all of us are profoundly affected by our experiences and personal histories. Some jurors, for example, have law enforcement members or prosecutors in their family; some have family members who have been arrested. When these relationships come to light during the jury selection process, we ask jurors if they will be able to make a fair decision based purely on the evidence presented, in spite of the fact they may have had some past experience with law enforcement (either positive or negative). My son, for example, became a juror (and even served as the foreman) in spite of the fact that his father and grandfather were detectives and a close family friend was a criminal prosecutor. Some people are able to put their feelings aside and some are not. If you can't remain open minded, you won't be able to serve on a jury. I want jurors who are capable of examining the evidence fairly, regardless of their relationships and past histories. I'm looking for open-minded jurors.

When Jesus selected His twelve apostles, He picked men who were open minded. They may have come from a sullied or questionable past, like the apostle Matthew, but their past life wasn't as important to Jesus as their present state of mind. Matthew was not a disciple of John the Baptist prior to meeting Jesus. Instead, he was a first-century tax collector (who may have been collecting taxes from the Jews for Herod Antipas). Tax collectors like Matthew were typically despised by the Jewish populace, who saw them as little more than traitors and thieves.[3] You might think that someone like this would be closed minded to the righteous teaching of Jesus, but this was not the case. Matthew was open to what Jesus had to say and even invited Jesus to his own home for dinner. Matthew left his life as a tax collector and eventually described his life with Jesus in the gospel bearing his name.

As a Christian case maker, I want to be as effective as possible, even though I know there are people who have deeply entrenched biases they are unwilling (or presently unable) to resist. Some people simply cannot be fair. It would be unwise to place a closed-minded person on a criminal jury, and it may be equally unwise to set your sights on someone like this as the *focus* of your Christian case making.

You've probably encountered your fair share of people who are hostile toward Christianity. Unlike apathetic jurors, people who are unwilling to evaluate our claims fairly have often had a bad experience with Christianity (or, more likely, with Christians). When I encounter people like this, I recognize my responsibility as yet another Christian they've encountered. Police officers understand that their actions are under constant scrutiny. In a world of smartphones and personal video devices, everything we do can be captured for closer examination.

Forensic Faith
Communication Guideline:

IDENTIFY THE "SEEKERS"

Sometimes it's easy to identify the "seekers" in your life—the people who are searching for the answers their worldview hasn't been able to provide. Sometimes it's more difficult to identify people who are starting to have questions.

If you've got young people in your life, start to ask them about the strength of their convictions. You'll be surprised to find they may be holding questions they haven't felt comfortable asking. Anticipate their questions given what you know about them. Create a question-asking environment.

For those you don't know as well, you may want to take a different approach to create a question-asking environment. We often focus on friends and family members who are not yet even curious about Christianity. Unsurprisingly, they may be difficult to reach. What can we do about it? Try living the kind of life that *causes* others to ask you about your beliefs. Are we reflecting the nature of Jesus to those around us? Are they even curious about what we believe? Start living in a way that provokes people to ask about the Christian worldview.

As a result, we've learned the importance of being a *consistent* and *persistent* ambassador for our profession and our agencies. As a Christian, I know I am also under the constant, watchful eye of my Master. Am I making Him proud? Am I contributing to the negative perception some atheists have of Christians? Is there something I can do to influence the nonbelievers in my world positively without compromising my role as an ambassador for God? I don't want to be yet another reason unbelievers dislike Christians; I don't want to aggravate the problem. I may still take the time to share what I believe, but I am more realistic in my expectations and more sensitive to what's really keeping them from seeing the truth.

Good Jurors Are Humble Jurors

I'm cautious about impaneling someone who has expertise in an area critical to our case. If we're going to call an electrical professional as an expert witness, for example, we probably shouldn't put an electrician on our jury. Why? Because time and time again, we've seen jurors become prideful when they encounter testimony within their discipline. Jurors who think they are experts in a particular field sometimes have difficulty accepting the testimony of *other* experts. It's often a matter of pride. Good decision making requires a degree of humility, and jurors who think they "know better" can make a mess of your case. I want jurors who are smart but teachable, jurors who won't allow their pride to stand in the way of the truth. I'm looking for humble jurors.

Humility was also important to Jesus. He was undoubtedly impressed with the humble nature he saw in Matthew, who accepted what Jesus had to say and repented from his prior sinful life as a tax collector. In fact, Jesus may have had Matthew in mind when He later told a story illustrating the importance of humility:

Luke 18:10–14

Two men went up into the temple to pray, one a Pharisee and the other a tax collector. The Pharisee stood and was praying this to himself: "God, I thank You that I am not like other people: swindlers, unjust, adulterers, or even like this tax collector. I fast twice a week; I pay tithes of all that I get." But the tax collector, standing some distance away, was even unwilling to lift up his eyes to heaven, but was beating his breast, saying, "God, be merciful to me, the sinner!" I tell you, this man went to his house justified rather than the other; for everyone who exalts himself will be humbled, but he who humbles himself will be exalted.

Jesus repeatedly told His followers to resist arrogance and pride. As a Christian case maker, I've come to recognize the relationship between *knowledge* and *pride*. As one increases, so can the other, and no one is exempt from this general rule (including me). The Internet has only complicated the matter for those of us who want to share the truth about Christianity. There's enough online information available to make just about anyone think they're an "expert" on any number of theological, scientific, or philosophical subjects, even though this information is often unvetted and unreliable. It can be difficult to share truth with people who errantly think they've already mastered a topic by simply surfing the web. These people aren't hard to spot; most of us recognize arrogance from a distance. When looking for opportunities to share, I try to identify people who are smart but teachable—people who won't allow their pride to stand in the way of the truth.

Jurors aren't the only ones in jeopardy from arrogant overconfidence. Case makers also place themselves at risk when we allow excessive pride to characterize our efforts. As the Bible accurately describes, "Pride goes before destruction, and a haughty spirit before stumbling" (Proverbs 16:18). When a detective takes the stand in a criminal case and comes off as arrogant or brash, his testimony is likely to be rejected by a jury. In a similar way, prosecutors and attorneys who appear haughty or self-important typically alienate the very jury they are trying to convince. If you're hoping to make the case for Christianity and encounter a prideful resister, take a minute to examine *your own* attitude. One sure way to amplify the pride of someone you're trying to reach is to allow *your own* arrogance to overtake *you*. When pride meets pride, nothing good results. If you can be humble, self-effacing, and gracious in your approach, you're far more likely to draw those characteristics out of the person you are trying to reach.

The 3/4 Principle

In an effort to help you identify and employ these important "jury" characteristics so you can decide where your efforts might be most effective, let me introduce you to something I call the "¾ Principle." In the many years I've been involved in criminal trials, I've learned there are two large groups from which juries are typically selected:

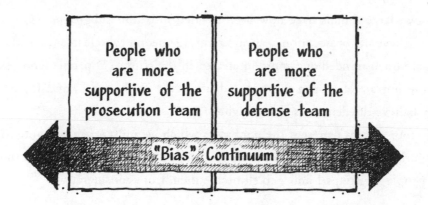

Our jury pool is filled with people who are either (1) more supportive of the prosecution team, or (2) more supportive of the defense team. Members of the first group may have had prior positive experiences with law enforcement—or they may have themselves been victims who benefited from the work of a prosecutor. Members of the second group may have had a negative experience with law enforcement or may know someone they think was falsely accused.

These two groups can be further divided into two subsets. If we create a "bias continuum" of sorts, we can chart these four subsets in the following way:

Our two large groups have now been divided into four subgroups: (1) people who inflexibly believe the prosecution is always right, (2) people who lean toward the prosecution but are open minded and more interested in the truth, (3) people who lean toward the defense but are also open minded and interested in the truth, and (4) people who inflexibly believe the defense is always right.

These four groups represent the pool from which we must select our potential jurors. The best juries are assembled from people in groups 2 and 3, so attorneys do their best to identify people in groups 1 and 4 to eliminate them from consideration.

Christian case makers can learn something from the bias continuum we've just examined. If you've spent much time sharing what you believe with your friends or family, you know they can also be divided into two distinct groups: (1) Christian believers, and (2) nonbelievers.

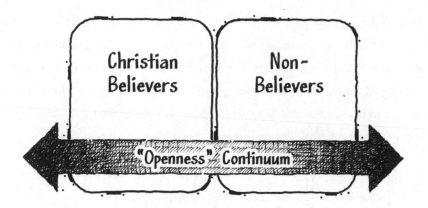

These two groups can be further divided into four subgroups: (1) believers who are convinced of their position, (2) believers who are starting to have doubts, (3) nonbelievers who are starting to have doubts, and (4) nonbelievers who are convinced of their position. These four groups can be placed in a "belief continuum" of sorts, from those who are most *convinced* (on the left), to those who are most *unconvinced* (on the right):

Members of these groups represent the "jury pool" from which we must select our potential "jurors." As a Christian case maker who has written books, speaks publicly, and continues to make the case for Christianity online, I've learned an important truth. Although I am writing and speaking to the members of all *four* groups, I know only *three* of these groups are open minded enough to listen to what I have to say. Members of groups 1, 2, and 3 are receptive, while members of group 4 typically are *not*:

It doesn't take long to identify where someone is positioned in this continuum. Sometimes you can discover where a person stands by simply being courageous enough to ask a few pointed questions. You probably already know what most members of your family believe, and if you're lucky enough to have outspoken friends or acquaintances online, their position may also be obvious. In any case, once you've determined where people are in this continuum, you'll be better able to decide how to proceed.

Group 1 – The Convinced Believer

You might not think there's any reason to share the evidence for Christianity with people who are already convinced Christianity is true, but nothing could be further from the truth.

This book, for example, was written *for Christians*. Those who are already convinced may not even be aware of the strong case supporting their beliefs, and they may not feel any need for evidence beyond their own personal experience of the risen Christ.

However, there's still good reason for people in this group to master the evidence. Chances are very good they've got someone in their immediate family who is struggling in group 2. Most of the parents who ask me for help with their skeptical children are themselves convinced that Christianity is true, even though their kids are not. How can we, as parents, respond to our kids' questions if we are not prepared with the evidence? If you're in group 1, it's still important to master the evidence so you can help your own children who may someday be in group 2. When I identify someone as a convinced Christian, I take the time to ask them if they are ready to help the people they know who are in groups 2 and 3. If they hold something other than a thoughtful, *forensic faith*, I make the case for a more evidential approach to their Christian belief. People in group 1 also need to hear (and master) the case.

Group 2 – The Doubting Believer

Many young Christians fall into group 2. They may have been raised in the church, but by the time they enter junior high or middle school, young Christians want to know more than *what* their parents believe: they want to know *why* their parents believe. If they don't get good answers at home, they'll be ready to accept *any* answer they get in school or college as they shift from *convinced* to *doubting* believers. I encounter young doubters all the time, and it's a privilege and honor to help them find their evidential footing. In my experience, Christian case makers can have the most impact with this second group, and all of us ought to be focused on the future of the church: young people.

Forensic Faith Definition:

BIAS

Everyone has an opinion, but not everyone holds a bias. Bias is typically defined as an unfair prejudice in favor of or against one view, person, or group when compared with another. While all of us have a personal preference, jurors are asked to avoid unfair prejudice.

Are there places in your life where your own bias has prevented you from sharing the truth about Christianity? Are there some groups you are simply unwilling to reach? As Christians, we often complain about the bias some people have against Christianity, but are we also harboring a bias against people we could otherwise reach? Read Mark 2:14–17 and examine the difference between the bias of the Pharisees and the attitude of Jesus. Are you more like the Pharisees or Jesus?

At my age, I can easily pick my peers. By the time you enter your fifties, you've probably surrounded yourself with people who are a lot like you. But young Christians, especially when they enter the largely hostile environment of the university, find themselves surrounded by people they *can't* select; many of these new peers are unfriendly to, or skeptical of, the claims of Christianity. That's why young Christians in group 2 need to be prepared with the evidence.

Group 3 – The Doubting Nonbeliever

I've received hundreds of emails and social media comments from nonbelievers who are beginning to question their nonbelief. Many of these group 3 seekers began by having serious doubts about their commitment to *naturalism*. When trying to account for some of the evidence I describe in *God's Crime Scene*, they discovered the insufficiency of their prior atheistic, naturalistic explanations.

Famed atheist Antony Flew found himself in such a position. Flew was an influential atheist and a self-identified evidentialist. He became a prominent spokesperson for atheism even as he attended C. S. Lewis's Socratic Club, and although he respected Lewis's work and character, he remained ambivalent to Lewis's arguments for Christianity. Flew believed that atheism should be everyone's default position until an evidential case for God could be made. He eventually began to question his atheism, however, as science provided him with the evidence he'd been looking for. Flew was particularly interested in the origin of information in DNA and the appearance of design in biological organisms. During this time of questioning, he was in contact (professionally and otherwise) with theists like Christian scholar Gary Habermas and author Roy Varghese. In fact, when Flew eventually abandoned his commitment to atheism, he coauthored a book with Varghese entitled *There Is a God: How the World's Most Notorious Atheist Changed His Mind*. Flew is an excellent example of the role good case making plays in reaching people in group 3.

Group 4 – The Convinced Nonbeliever

If you've ever expressed your Christian beliefs on social media, you may have come into contact with someone in group 4. In the early 2000s, spurred by a number of aggressive atheist writers like Christopher Hitchens, Sam Harris, Richard Dawkins, and Daniel Dennett, a movement that's been referred to as "New Atheism" emerged. While the arguments offered by these writers were not innovative or unique, their approach was far more hostile and targeted than ever before. *New Atheism* is all about a *new attitude*. Many (but not all) people in group 4 have adopted the approach of the New Atheists, and you'll observe this in their aggressive interaction. They are convinced of the rationality of their position, and even more importantly, they are equally convinced of the irrationality of Christian belief. They can be sarcastic, condescending, and mean spirited. Until a person in group 4 migrates into group 3, he or she will be far more likely to abuse Christian case makers than listen to the Christian case.

Jesus recognized the nature of people in this fourth group. Matthew described an occasion when Jesus visited His hometown of Nazareth (in Matthew 13:53–58). Jesus met resistance from people who simply refused to accept His claims. In fact, they got angry with Jesus and "took offense at Him." According to Matthew, the resistance of these "group four" convinced unbelievers was reflected in Jesus's approach: "He did not do many miracles there because of their unbelief" (verse 58).

I make the case to people in all four groups, but once I identify someone is in group 4, I intensify an important aspect of my approach. I *pray* for them and continue to *love* them in spite of our differences. There are people I care for deeply who are still committed members of group 4. I was also a member of this group for most of my life. Only after God removed my enmity was I ready to hear what people had to say about Him. Once I became a Christian, several of my Christian friends and coworkers told me they had been praying for me for *years*. I remained connected to these people during my years of unbelief because they continued to demonstrate the love of God to me through their actions and words. They never gave up; they loved me

Forensic Faith
Communication Guideline:
ORGANIZE YOUR "JURORS"

We've been talking about the importance of lists; this discipline of list making can help us reach our friends and family. Make a list of all the people you'd like to reach with the evidence for Christianity. We typically include only nonbelievers in a list like this, but now you know why it's important to include people from all four groups.

Once you've assembled your list, start to think about the group categories we've described. After identifying the group to which each person belongs, begin to think about the appropriate response and strategy for everyone on your list. Who needs to be convinced of the importance of a forensic faith? Who is struggling with their Christian belief and needs an evidential foundation? Who is seeking answers as an atheist and needs to be exposed to the evidence for God? Who is still in adamant rebellion and simply needs prayer? Make a list and take action.

unconditionally. Whenever I become frustrated with people in group 4 who are unreceptive to Christianity, I ask myself, "When was the last time I prayed for this person and asked God to remove this hostility? Have I been showing them how much I care about them, or have I been distancing myself from them just because we disagree?" I've learned to pray and love my friends and family members who are still part of group 4. I'm watching for God's activity in their lives and waiting for an opportunity to be a good Christian case maker.

The 3/4 Principle has helped me set more reasonable goals and temper my expectations when sharing what I believe with others. Once I understand where people are positioned, I'm better able to select passionate, open-minded, and humble "jurors."

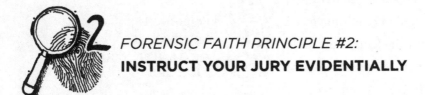

FORENSIC FAITH PRINCIPLE #2:
INSTRUCT YOUR JURY EVIDENTIALLY

Jesus didn't simply *select* the right twelve men to be His apostles; He *instructed* them specifically so they could better perform their mission. Jesus taught many people over the course of His three-year ministry, but the disciples received *special* instruction. When the crowds had difficulty understanding His parables, Jesus instructed the twelve disciples to help them comprehend the meaning of each story and analogy (see Matthew 13:1–51). Prior to sending the disciples out to share what they had learned, Jesus instructed them specifically in the manner in which they should travel, engage nonbelievers, and discuss the truth (see Matthew 10:1–23). Jesus chose His disciples carefully and instructed them before entrusting them with the truth.

Criminal jurors are in similar need of instruction. I've been present for many *voir dire* sessions, and I've discovered something interesting: during this selection process, attorneys learn a lot about *jurors*, but jurors also learn a lot about the *nature of evidence*. Attorneys question potential jurors about what they know related to certain aspects of evidence, and this questioning often serves as a form of *instruction*.

The *voir dire* process isn't the only place where jurors learn about the nature of evidence and the role it plays in assessing truth claims. As evidence is presented at trial, and certainly as the attorneys make their closing arguments, jurors become familiar, either directly or indirectly, with the basic rules of evidence and the nature of good case making. Then, just before jurors are released to deliberate on what they've seen and heard, judges provide *specific* directions to help the jury evaluate the evidence. Every state has "Jury Instructions" that are part of the criminal code.

Criminal jurors benefit deeply from this education, and they aren't the only evaluators who need to be taught about the nature and role of evidence. The people who hear the case for Christianity could also benefit from some evidential instruction. Richard Dawkins (one of the aforementioned New Atheists), for example, once wrote:

> Many of us saw religion as harmless nonsense. Beliefs might lack all supporting evidence but, we thought, if people needed a crutch for consolation, where's the harm? September 11th changed all that.[4]

When someone claims Christian (or theistic beliefs) "lack all supporting evidence," either they aren't familiar with the large body of evidence related to Christianity or they aren't familiar with what *qualifies* as evidence in the first place. If we hope to offer something evidentially persuasive, we'll need to instruct people in the nature and role of evidence *prior* to citing the evidence itself. The following attributes of evidence are important to jurors assessing criminal cases, and they're also important to people making and evaluating the case for Christianity.

EVIDENCE INSTRUCTION #1:
THE FACT THE OTHER SIDE CAN MAKE A CASE DOESN'T MEAN IT'S TRUE

In *Cold-Case Christianity*, I wrote an entire chapter entitled "Prepare for an Attack." In this chapter, I described many of the strategies defense attorneys take when attempting to counter the prosecution's case. If there's one thing every Christian case maker needs to understand about the opposition's response, it's this: don't be shocked that the other side can make a seemingly persuasive argument. The fact the opposition can make a case doesn't mean it's true.

I've heard many stories from young Christians (like the one I cited in chapter 1) who entered the university only to discover a professor who could make a powerful presentation in support of his or her atheistic worldview. Many times, these presentations were openly hostile to the claims of Christianity. Some of these young Christian students, unfamiliar with the objections of atheists, heard this opposing case for the very first time presented authoritatively from the professor's podium. The impact was dramatic. The opposition offered an articulate, seemingly reasonable presentation, and having never heard such an argument, the Christians in the classroom were caught off guard and unprepared.

Forensic Faith
Communication Guideline:

GET FAMILIAR WITH THE OPPOSITION

It's easy to live in isolation of people who hold a different view of the world. As a Christian, have you surrounded yourself with like-minded friends and acquaintances? You might be surprised to see or read the level of venom waiting on the Internet for those who want to share the gospel.

There's a way to sample the arguments and disposition of the opposition safely. Start by joining an atheist group on Facebook, Reddit, or another similar social media platform. You can join these groups without having to engage any of the content, but while you're there, take the time to read what they're saying. If you've never dipped your toes into the debate, you'll get a chance to see what's happening on the "front lines." Remember though: the fact the other side can make a case doesn't mean it's true.

Think back for a minute to the case I described earlier. Michael Lubahn's defense attorney sat patiently through the prosecution's presentation of evidence, even though it took weeks to complete. When the prosecutor rested, Lubahn's attorney got to work. He presented his own case, made his own argument, and was just as passionate as the prosecutor. In fact, no one was more certain of Michael Lubahn's innocence than his defense attorney, and he did his best to deliver an articulate, reasonable argument. Lubahn was convicted in spite of his attorney's noble effort, and as I described earlier, Michael confessed to the murder at his sentencing hearing. Although his attorney was capable of making a case, the mere fact he made one didn't make it true.

I've learned to expect a strong case from the opposition, but I know an *argument* is not *evidence*; a *presentation* is not a *refutation*. In fact, juries are specifically instructed about this:

> Nothing that the attorneys say is evidence. In their opening statements and closing arguments, the attorneys will discuss the case, but their remarks are not evidence. Their questions are not evidence. Only the witnesses' answers are evidence. The attorneys' questions are significant only if they help you

understand the witnesses' answers. Do not assume that something is true just because one of the attorneys asks a question that suggests it is true.[5]

This is an important rule of evidence: don't assume something is true just because someone with authority says it, suggests it, or makes a case for it. Expect an aggressive rebuttal, and remember that a presentation is not a refutation. Examine the evidence for yourself. Connect the dots. Use your common sense.

EVIDENCE INSTRUCTION #2:
EVERYTHING HAS THE POTENTIAL TO BE EVIDENCE

Many people simply don't understand the basic categories of evidence (as I described earlier) and mistakenly think prosecutors need a particular *kind* of evidence to be successful. This simply isn't true. Must we have DNA or fingerprint evidence to determine if a suspect was involved in the crime? No. Must we have a witness to prove a suspect is involved in the crime? No again. As I described in chapter 1, direct evidence is limited to eyewitness testimony. Indirect evidence (also known as circumstantial evidence) is everything else. When I say "everything else," I mean precisely that: *everything* has the potential to be considered as evidence. In our criminal cases, we've presented physical objects, statements, behaviors, and much more. Take, for example, another look at the list of potential evidences I listed in chapter 3 (on page 102). *Everything* must be considered for its evidential value when investigating a crime; sometimes the simplest detail can make the case. As I described earlier, I've been involved with successfully prosecuted cases that consisted of nothing more than statements.

When skeptics say the case for Christianity is weak because it can't be built with scientific, testable, physical, forensic evidence, they simply don't know how criminal cases are tried every day in America. That's why we need to help people understand: *Everything* counts as evidence, including the behavior of the original witnesses; the testimony of those who listened to the statements of these witnesses; the corroborative evidence of archaeology; the internal confirmation of geography, politics, and proper nouns; and the deficiency of alternative explanations. These forms of evidence (or something very similar) are used in criminal trials every day.

If convictions were dependent on physical, forensic evidence, very few cases would ever be prosecuted. What qualifies as evidence? Everything.

EVIDENCE INSTRUCTION #3:
WHOEVER MAKES THE CLAIM HAS THE BURDEN OF PROOF

Gratefully, people in our country are afforded the presumption of innocence in legal trials. Defendants are presumed innocent until proven guilty, and the standard of proof (the SOP) is much higher in criminal trials than it is in civil trials. The "burden of proof," the responsibility to prove the defendant is guilty of an offense, lies with the prosecutor who filed the criminal complaint. The prosecutor, after all, is the one who is making the claim of guilt; therefore, the burden is on him or her to prove his or her case. Criminal jury instructions describe this burden:

> The fact that a criminal charge has been filed against the defendant[s] is not evidence that the charge is true. You must not be biased against the defendant[s] just because (he/she/they) (has/have) been arrested, charged with a crime, or brought to trial. A defendant in a criminal case is presumed to be innocent. This presumption requires that the People prove a defendant guilty beyond a reasonable doubt. Whenever I tell you the People must prove something, I mean they must prove it beyond a reasonable doubt [unless I specifically tell you otherwise].[6]

This "burden of proof" principle is often applied to those of us who make claims about the existence of God. Most atheists believe we, as theists, have the *sole* burden of proof. A popular atheist website describes it in the following way:

> The burden of proof falls on whoever makes a positive claim. If I claim the Flying Spaghetti Monster exists, it is not your duty to disprove me. In fact, that might be impossible. Rather, it is my duty to back up my claim with reasons and evidence. If you claim that Yahweh exists, it's not my duty to disprove Yahweh.[7]

According to many atheists, Christians are making a positive claim about an invisible Being; the evidential burden is ours to shoulder. I would agree somewhat with this assessment, but I also recognize its limits, given my experience as an investigator.

When detectives enter a crime scene, we are presented with a collection of evidence that must be explained if we hope to determine the ultimate cause of the crime. Detectives sometimes disagree about the best explanation for the evidence or the identity of the suspect. When that happens, we assemble in our conference room and make the case to one another, arguing for the suspect (or cause) we believe best explains the evidence. In that room, each and every detective has the burden of convincing the others that his or her explanation is the best. The burden of proof is shared by everyone who offers a potential "cause" for the evidence in the crime scene.

Forensic Faith
Communication Guideline:
REQUIRE MORE OF THE OTHER SIDE

We typically jump to defend what we believe about God's existence and the truth of Christianity without stopping to ask the other side how they can account for the universe *without* God. Discussions about "religion" or "spiritual matters" have the potential of being one-sided defenses of God's existence.

Next time you're in a conversation about such matters, turn the dialogue, instead, into a defense of *naturalism*. Ask your skeptical friends to explain how everything we see in the universe (particularly the eight pieces of evidence I describe in *God's Crime Scene*) can be explained by employing nothing more than space, time, matter, and the laws that govern such things. Shift the burden of proof, and require more from the opposition.

In a similar way, the universe is filled with evidence that must be explained. How did the universe come into being from nothing? Why does the universe appear to be fine-tuned for life? How did life originate from non-living materials? Why do biological organisms appear designed? How did immaterial consciousness emerge from material processes? How is free agency possible in a purely physical, deterministic universe? What establishes the transcendent, objective, moral truths we all recognize and employ? What is the transcendent standard of "good" we reference when describing the existence of true "evil"? These eight questions represent eight important pieces of evidence in the universe. These realities must be explained just like the evidence in any crime scene.

As it turns out, there are only two possible categories of explanation for the evidence we see in the universe: (1) naturalistic explanations employing nothing more than space, time, matter, and the laws of physics or chemistry that govern such things; or (2) supernatural explanations that employ the existence of a supernatural Being. Atheists believe naturalism can best account for the evidence in the universe; theists (i.e., Christians) believe God is the best explanation. Like detectives in the conference room, each group has an *equal* burden of proof to demonstrate their "suspect" is the best explanation.

If you're going to make claims about God's existence to your nonbelieving friends or family members, be prepared with the evidence needed to make your case. But remember, atheists must also explain what we observe and experience in the universe, and they share an equal evidential burden. Make sure they are called to defend *their* position, even as they require you to defend *yours*.

EVIDENCE INSTRUCTION #4:
POSSIBILITIES ARE IRRELEVANT

There's a reason why the standard of proof in criminal trials is "beyond a *reasonable* doubt," rather than "beyond a *possible* doubt." If prosecutors had to establish a defendant's guilt beyond a *possible* doubt, no one would ever be convicted of a crime. Most jury instructions recognize the fact that there will always be some form of possible or imaginary doubt, even when jurors return a guilty verdict in a criminal trial:

> Whenever I tell you the People must prove something, I mean they must prove it beyond a reasonable doubt [unless I specifically tell you otherwise]. Proof beyond a reasonable doubt is proof that leaves you with an abiding conviction that the charge is true. The evidence need not eliminate all possible doubt because everything in life is open to some possible or imaginary doubt.[8]

When questioning jurors during *voir dire*, it's not uncommon for prosecutors to ask, "Are you the kind of person who can't make a decision unless every possible question has been answered?" If potential jurors say they can't make a decision in the midst of unanswered possibilities, they'll be excused from jury duty.

In addition, jurors, once they hear all the evidence in a case, are typically instructed to refrain from speculating about what they *don't know*. Instead, they are instructed to focus on what they *do know*, given what they saw and heard during the course of the trial:

> You may draw reasonable inferences from the evidence which you feel are justified in the light of common experience, keeping in mind that such inferences should not be based on speculation or guess.[9]

Jurors are asked to make "reasonable inferences" from the evidence and to resist the temptation to speculate about "possibilities."

This is also good advice for those of us who are evaluating the reasonable explanations for the evidence in the universe. You'd be surprised to see how much *speculation* masquerades as *reasonable inference*, especially in theories related to the origin of the universe. Most of us are familiar with "multiverse theories" that have been offered to explain the fine-tuning we see in the universe. You may also be familiar with "string theories" (related to the nature of quantum physics) that have been offered to explain the origin of the universe.

Both of these naturalistic theories (as I describe in *God's Crime Scene*) are popular among atheists, but they are highly *speculative*. These theories are contested by both theistic and atheistic physicists for their lack of evidential support. Are the theories *possible*? Absolutely. Anything is *possible*. But are they evidentially *reasonable*? No. When talking with your skeptical friends about the existence of God, take some time to ask them why they aren't skeptical about some of the evidentially unsupported theories promoted by those who *deny* the existence of God. Remember: possibilities are irrelevant; evidentially reasonable inferences *aren't*.

EVIDENCE INSTRUCTION #5:
THE MORE CUMULATIVE THE CASE, THE MORE REASONABLE THE CONCLUSION

I'm occasionally asked, "Jim, what was the one piece of evidence that convinced you Christianity was true? When did you have that 'aha moment'?" When people ask questions like this, I think they are hoping to identify a single "silver bullet" piece of evidence they

Forensic Faith Communication Guideline:

PRACTICE CUMULATIVE CASE MAKING

When you stop and think about it, all of us have experience as cumulative case makers. We do it all the time, without even thinking about the evidential principle we're employing. Next time you're thinking about your job, hobby, loved one, or an item in the local news, practice your cumulative case-making abilities so you'll be ready to make a comprehensive case for what you believe as a Christian.

Here are a few examples: Why do you think your favorite sports team will (or won't) make the playoffs next year? Assemble a six-point cumulative case. Think about your current position at work. Make a five-point case for why you did (or didn't) get promoted the last time you had the opportunity. If you own a dog or cat, make an eight-point cumulative case for why this breed is (or isn't) a good breed to own. In each of these examples, recognize the power of multiple evidences when making a case for what you believe.

Return to chapter 1 and review the section on the "evidential emissaries" so you'll be prepared to make the case for the eyewitness status of the gospel authors. Can you offer three or four reasons why the earliest Christians believed the authors of the Gospels were, in fact, eyewitnesses? When you're ready, review the four-part eyewitness reliability template in *Cold-Case Christianity* so you can take the extra step of defending the reliability of the gospel eyewitnesses.

might use to persuade others. I hate to disappoint them, but my honest answer is: "There wasn't one piece of evidence that convinced me Christianity was true."

There were hundreds of pieces. That's the nature of all my criminal cases as well. When we first began working cold cases as an agency, a partner on the homicide team brought me a case he thought was promising. He had a particular suspect in mind and was disappointed when I remained unconvinced. But after two years of additional investigation, I knew we had the right suspect in our sights. Why? Because we gathered dozens of additional pieces of evidence and these new evidences all pointed to the same suspect. The more cumulative the case, the more reasonable the conclusion.

I am a huge fan of cumulative cases. They are *the* most effective way to demonstrate something is true. When the standard of proof is "beyond a reasonable doubt," jurors are far more comfortable when the case is *overwhelming*. That's why we take the time to collect, list, and demonstrate how *many* pieces of evidence point to a defendant. The more the evidence amasses against a particular suspect, the shorter the jury deliberation.

Cumulative cases also help us understand how to interpret single, less obvious pieces of evidence. Let's say, for example, a suspect behaves in a certain way the day after a murder. It's my job to determine if that behavior is an indication of guilt, but there are times when a behavior can be confusing and may not be interpreted as an indication of guilt. So how should I (and later, the jury) interpret this behavior? The other pieces of evidence in the cumulative case can guide us to the correct interpretation. If ninety-nine pieces of evidence are best interpreted as evidence of guilt and one piece of evidence seems confusing, I allow the ninety-nine pieces to inform the one rather than allow the one piece of evidence to inform the ninety-nine.

When we make the case for what we believe as Christians, we need to instruct people on this simple, foundational principle. Let's say, for example, we are attempting to make the biblical case for a particular doctrine or theological truth. We begin by collecting the evidence in the case: all the biblical verses that address the issue under investigation. Some of these verses will have more than one reasonable interpretation. How will we know which interpretation is correct? By referring to the *cumulative case*. If ninety-nine verses are best interpreted to support a particular biblical truth and one verse seems confusing, I allow the ninety-nine verses to inform the one, rather than allow the one verse to inform the ninety-nine.

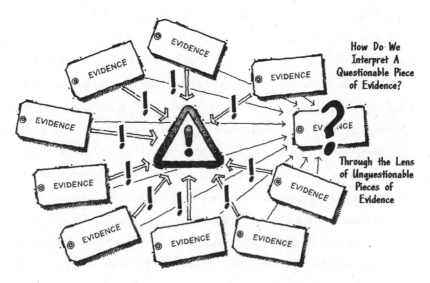

How Do We Interpret A Questionable Piece of Evidence?

Through the Lens of Unquestionable Pieces of Evidence

Let's take a look at an example from a single passage in James's epistle that some have used to argue our salvation is dependent on "good works":

> **James 2:14, 21–26** (ESV)
> What good is it, my brothers, if someone says he has faith but does not have works? Can that faith save him? … Was not Abraham our father justified by works when he offered up his son Isaac on the altar? You see that faith was active along with his works, and faith was completed by his works; and the Scripture was fulfilled that says, "Abraham believed God, and it was counted to him as righteousness"—and he was called a friend of God. You see that a person is justified by works and not by faith alone. And in the same way was not also Rahab the prostitute justified by works when she received the messengers and sent them out by another way? For as the body apart from the spirit is dead, so also faith apart from works is dead.

How are we to interpret this passage? It sounds like James is saying our salvation is dependent on our effort to obey the Law and perform "good works." But if that's the case, James's teaching appears to be in conflict with a rich, robust, cumulative case for salvation by faith *alone* (i.e., John 3:16; Acts 16:31; Romans 3:28–30; 4:5; 5:1; 9:30; 10:4; 11:6; Galatians 2:8–9, 16, 21; 3:5–6, 24; Ephesians 1:13; 2:8-9; Philippians 3:9; and Titus 3:5). These latter passages emphatically proclaim that "man is justified by faith *apart* from works of the Law (Romans 3:28), and that "to the one who does *not* work, but believes in Him who justifies the ungodly, his faith is credited as righteousness" (Romans 4:5). If we want to interpret James's single passage properly, we need to allow the many verses we find in Scripture to inform the one we find here, rather than allow the one verse to inform the many. When read in the context of the larger chapter (remember Greg Koukl's advice to "Never read a Bible verse"), James appears to be saying that we are saved not by our good works but by the *kind of faith* that *produces* good works. That's a critical distinction. According to James, there are *two kinds* of faith: one that leads to a godly life and good works and one that doesn't. One is "dead," while the other is "alive." This interpretation is reasonable given the many verses that describe salvation by faith alone.

If we want to become effective Christian case makers, we need to help people understand the overwhelming nature of the evidence for whatever we claim. The lists and summaries we described in the last chapter are excellent examples of how this can be done, but there is one downside to this approach: it requires us to be familiar and facile enough with the evidence to assemble good cumulative cases. That's why it's important to start disciplining yourself as a list maker. Cumulative cases are worth your time and energy.

EVIDENCE INSTRUCTION #6:

WITNESSES ARE RELIABLE UNLESS DEMONSTRATED OTHERWISE

Much has been written about the reliability (or unreliability) of eyewitnesses over the years. When a witness provides information in support of an attorney's position, the attorney is likely to argue the witness should be trusted. On the other hand, if a witness provides information detrimental to the attorney's case, the attorney will probably argue against the reliability of this witness (or eyewitnesses in general). I've been helped and harmed by eye-witnesses, so I've learned an important lesson: test your eyewitnesses and trust them—*if* they pass the test.

In *Cold-Case Christianity*, I outline a simple four-part template (derived from the California Jury Instructions) for evaluating eyewitnesses. If it can be established that (1) a witness was actually present to see the event, (2) can be corroborated (even in a limited way) by another witness or additional evidence, (3) has not changed his story but has been honest and accurate over time, and (4) doesn't possess a bias that might cause him to lie, you are to consider the witness reliable.

When making the case for Christianity to your nonbelieving friends and family, take the time to explain why you trust the accounts in the Gospels. Learn enough about these four aspects of eyewitness reliability to be able to instruct others, and help them understand an important truth: an eyewitness can be *wrong* about a particular detail and still be considered *reliable*. Jury instructions typically reference this fact:

> Do not automatically reject testimony just because of inconsistencies or conflicts. Consider whether the differences are important or not. People

sometimes honestly forget things or make mistakes about what they remember. Also, two people may witness the same event yet see or hear it differently.[10]

As a Christian, I affirm the inerrancy of Scripture. I don't believe the authors of the Gospels are wrong about any of their claims, and I don't believe there is an error in the biblical text, even if there may appear to be "contradictions" to those who are unfamiliar with eyewitness testimony. But when making the case to those who are critical of eyewitness evidence, I "lower the bar" a bit and provide them with the jury instruction I've described above. Given this legal instruction, even if I didn't believe the Gospels were error-free, I'd *still* have to conclude they're *reliable* and *trustworthy*.

Forensic Faith
Communication Guideline:
MAKE THE CASE FOR EYEWITNESS STATUS

Skeptics of the Gospels typically refuse to allow the Gospels to be described as eyewitness accounts, because they prefer to think of them as *fictional tales*. That's another reason why it's important for us to be prepared with an evidential view of the gospel authors and a *forensic faith*.

Return to chapter 1 and review the section on the "Evidential Emissaries" so you'll be prepared to make the case for the eyewitness status of the gospel authors. Can you offer three or four reasons why the earliest Christians believed the authors of the Gospels were, in fact, eyewitnesses? When you're ready, review the four-part eyewitness reliability template in *Cold-Case Christianity* so you can take the extra step of defending the reliability of the gospel eyewitnesses.

Help the people you're trying to reach learn how to evaluate eyewitnesses. Along the way, take the time to instruct them about three important attributes of *true, reliable* eyewitnesses. While these characteristics may seem "troubling" at first, they are just the opposite:

Reliable Eyewitnesses Seldom Appear to Agree

Perspective is important, and it's not just one's physical proximity that determines what a witness did or didn't see. When you're staring down the barrel of a robber's pistol, you have a tendency to miss certain details that are picked up by the witness who is watching from across the room. There are many factors that contribute to one's perception of an event, including physical location, past experience, familiarity with a feature of the crime scene, and one's physical, emotional, or psychological condition. No two people are alike, so no two people experience an event in precisely the same way. Don't panic; that's normal. In fact, if three different witnesses tell you precisely the same thing, be suspicious.

Reliable Eyewitnesses Raise Questions

As I mentioned in the last chapter, witnesses often raise as many questions as they answer. We see this in criminal trials, and I demonstrated it in the biblical accounts as well. That's why multiple witnesses are so valuable, especially when they bring nuanced, perspectival differences to the case, providing "unintentional eyewitness support" for one another. So don't fret over the differences. Instead, *employ* the differences to gain a better understanding of what happened. There are times when differing accounts actually give us *greater* understanding and confidence.

Reliable Eyewitnesses Are Sometimes Incorrect

I've seen this repeatedly over the course of my career. Witnesses are people, and people make mistakes. I've never met an "inerrant eyewitness"; everyone is wrong about *something*. If inerrant witnesses were required to convict defendants, we'd never be able to prosecute *anyone* for *anything*. When examining the reliability of an eyewitness and encountering some factual error, take the time to (1) determine if the errant aspect of the statement is relevant to the larger issues in the case and (2) understand why the witness got the detail wrong in the first place. Is there a reason why the stress of the situation may have caused the victim to be mistaken about a detail? Does the error change the overall validity of the testimony or make a difference to the larger nature of the case? Are there additional sources we can consult to remedy the discrepancy? Take the time to resolve the issue before jettisoning the testimony.

If you teach your "jurors" about the nature of eyewitnesses before you offer the gospel eyewitness accounts, you'll remove objections before they arise and lay the foundation for why you trust what the Bible has to say about Jesus.

Jurors receive indirect instruction from the attorneys and direct instruction from the judge over the course of a criminal trial. Without this instruction, the jurors would be unable to understand what qualifies as evidence or how to evaluate this evidence when making a decision. Your hearers are in no less need of instruction. Take the time to learn about the nature of evidence so you can pass on what you've learned to others as part of your case-making process. Instruct your "jury."

FORENSIC FAITH PRINCIPLE #3:
MAKE AN OPENING STATEMENT ENTHUSIASTICALLY

I'll never forget a case I had many years ago involving a new district attorney in his first year trying felony cases. He was exceptionally bright and articulate. During the preparation for the trial, I grew increasingly excited about what this young attorney might be able to do in front of a jury. My expectations were crushed, however, once he stepped behind the podium and began his opening statement.

It's one thing to be intellectually capable or academically prepared, but it's another to confidently and enthusiastically deliver what you've prepared to an audience. In a famous Gallup poll that asked Americans what they were afraid of, the fear of public speaking ranked second, just below the fear of snakes and just above the fear of heights.[11] My young attorney colleague can attest to the difficulty many people have when trying to communicate what they believe to others, especially in the opening minutes.

Along the way, however, I met many great orators in the district attorney's office, and one of my best friends, Deputy District Attorney John Lewin, is perhaps the finest communicator I know. But he wasn't always a confident, enthusiastic speaker. In fact, I met John very early in both of our careers. *His* first big cases were *my* first big cases. I watched him develop as a communicator over the years, and I can now tell you what makes him great. Every jury trial begins with an opening statement from both attorneys, and John specializes in the art of "first impressions." His enthusiastic opening statements garner the respect and attention of the jury *immediately*.

Jesus's "opening statements" were the best ever delivered. No one captured the attention and imagination of an audience like Jesus did. His followers were inspired, even as His adversaries were challenged and convicted. One day, while sitting with James, John, and Andrew on the Mount of Olives, Jesus began to tell His disciples about the future:

> See to it that no one misleads you. Many will come in My name, saying, "I am He!" and will mislead many. When you hear of wars and rumors of wars, do not be frightened; those things must take place; but that is not yet the end. For nation will rise up against nation, and kingdom against kingdom; there will be earthquakes in various places; there will also be famines. These things are merely the beginning of birth pangs. (Mark 13:5–8)

Wow, do you think *that* opening statement got the attention of Jesus's disciples? Those were the *first* words of what has come to be known as the Olivet Discourse, one of the most famous and powerful of Jesus's sermons. Jesus started His presentation dramatically because He understood the power of a good "opening statement."

As a Christian case maker, I don't expect to craft an opening like Jesus. I'll settle for something closer to what John Lewin has been able to accomplish in his career as a prosecutor. If you're willing to learn from John and other attorneys like him, you can improve your "opening statements" dramatically.

Practice Your Presentation

John became better the more he worked at it. Unsurprising, right? Most of us recognize the value of *practice*. John practiced his craft indirectly, even when he wasn't in front of a jury. He and I met dozens of

Forensic Faith Communication Guideline:

FIND A PLACE TO PRACTICE

When I was an inexperienced Christian case maker, I looked for opportunities to practice in front of the smallest audience possible. So I started in the car, *by myself.* I listened to cassette tapes and CDs from accomplished Christian apologists, particularly debates featuring Christians and nonbelievers. After one side would finish presenting, I would turn off the audio and either practice responding to the argument I just heard or practice repeating what I had just heard.

Find a place to practice. Either practice in your car, by yourself, like I did, or start interacting with friends across the dinner table. Start small and think big. The more you learn in the privacy of your own thoughts or car, the better you'll be in front of your friends and family members.

times before each jury trial, discussing the evidence and the best way to present it. In these sessions, we discussed a variety of ways he might make the opening statement. John mulled over his possible approaches, refining them and taking input from me, his harshest (but most affirming) "critic." He knew he could trust me, and as we bantered back and forth over the importance of specific pieces of evidence, John's statement was refined and perfected.

There are lots of ways you can practice presenting the case for Christianity. Long before I ever began speaking publicly, I began refining my presentation skills informally with a close friend, Dirk Ringstad, at my dinner table. I knew I could trust Dirk as *my* harshest (but most affirming) "critic." We spent hours mulling over doctrines of Christianity and the value of specific Christian evidences. My young sons would listen to us debate and "practice" the case, and they still talk about it to this day. If you're eager to refine your communication skills, start *now*. Begin with case-making conversations, then, when you're ready, volunteer to teach a class at your church or lead a small group. Every setting is an opportunity to *practice*. The more you talk, teach, and lead, the more you'll see your skills develop and grow.

Protect Your First Impression

John understands the power of a first impression, and he knows it doesn't start at the opening statement. By the time the jurors get to hear about the case in John's opening, they've already spent many hours watching and listening to him. Jurors are a captive audience, and they watch the attorneys throughout the jury selection process, in the halls prior to their selection, and during every break along the way. John knows the eyes and ears of the jury are constantly pointed in his direction, so he's careful not to do or say anything that would jeopardize his ability to connect with them.

Your "jury" is also watching you long before you ever get the chance to share what you know to be true about Jesus. I hope you've protected your first impression, because you've already started to make it. Have you been the kind of person your friends and family members would *want* to listen to? Has your life been consistent with your message? Your first impression is critical to your success, and it starts a lot earlier than you think. If you've already damaged a relationship with someone you are trying to reach, take the time to admit your failings, repair broken relationships, and start anew before launching into your "opening statement." For those you still want to reach, remember you're *already* reaching them, even though you haven't yet started sharing what you know about Jesus.

Be Eager and Prepared

John *loves* opening statements. He's genuinely excited to start the trial and eager to tell the story. For John, the early moments in front of a jury are invigorating; he's not afraid or anxious. Why? Because by this time in the process, he knows the case as well as anyone on the planet, and he knows exactly how he's going to start telling it to the jury. John is *prepared* and his preparation results in *enthusiasm*.

As a Christian case maker, I know it's not always easy to get started. Spiritual conversations can be intimidating. One way to overcome your anxiety is to do what John does: master the case and know how you want to start. I met a young man many years ago named James Boccardo. He wrote a book entitled *Unsilenced: How to Voice the Gospel.* James was a consummate spiritual conversation starter. His fearless approach to opening statements rivaled John's; James was enthusiastic and eager. Why? Because he knew exactly how he was going to start a conversation, and he was ready to answer any question that came his way. James almost always started his conversations by finding a way to ask a version of the following question: "So, what do you think happens to you when you die?" That simple, brief question would typically start much longer conversations about the nature of life, afterlife, and the existence of God. James mastered all the possible responses to the question prior to starting so he was ready to provide an answer regardless of which direction the conversation veered (see his book to learn more).[12] James was *eager* because he was *prepared*.

I recently met a man at a speaking engagement in Montana who had a different, but equally effective, "opening statement." Grover Peterson has been involved in thousands of spiritual conversations and has led many people to Christ. He's eager and courageous when starting these conversations with strangers because he has his own prepared "opening statement." Grover usually approaches people and points out something in their immediate environment that's clearly designed (like a watch or ball-point pen). He then starts by saying, "Everything in life has a design, function, and purpose. What is *yours*?" This simple, engaging, inoffensive opening has given Grover an opportunity to start a number of spiritual conversations. Some of these help people start thinking about the design and purpose of life; some result in a presentation of the gospel. Grover is eager to deliver his opening statement because he is *prepared*.

Make Promises You Can Deliver

One of the most important things I've learned from John Lewin over the years is the value of *keeping your promises*. When John delivers his opening statement, he thoroughly presents what he knows about the case and the reason why the evidence points to the defendant's guilt. John's opening statement is, in essence, a *promise*. John makes a claim about the defendant, then pledges to back up his claim with evidence over the course of the trial. But John knows he can't make promises he can't later keep. He doesn't overstate his case because he knows he has to *deliver*. If he keeps his promises, he's got an excellent chance to be successful.

If you're getting ready to make the case for Christianity to your friends or family members, make sure you can deliver on your promises. Never cite something from the Internet you haven't thoroughly investigated for yourself. Expect your audience to fact-check everything you say, and do your best to be ready with your sources. Also, be careful not to overstate your case. The evidence supporting Christianity is strong enough without embellishment. If one of our juries was to catch John Lewin exaggerating about a single piece of evidence, they might rightly wonder if he also exaggerated about other issues (and simply hadn't been caught). Knowing this, John never overstates

Forensic Faith
Communication Guideline:
MEMORIZE YOUR "MOMENTUM STATEMENT"

If you've been making the case for Christianity with nonbelievers, you've probably noticed how easy it is to gravitate toward prior successes. Once we discover a successful approach, we're inclined to do something similar the next time around, especially when it comes to talking to someone about Christianity.

Take advantage of this inclination. Think about momentum and what you can do to achieve it in your opening words. Some people refer to this as "an elevator pitch": Imagine you're in the elevator with someone you're trying to convince on the way to the tenth floor. You've got one short opportunity to make your case persuasively. How will you open? Think about your options and what's been successful in the past, then memorize your approach (even write it down) so you can practice and improve it.

his case. He doesn't want to erode the confidence of his hearers. In a similar way, it's important for us to retain a sense of evidential modesty when making the case for Christianity; it will help us gain the trust of our hearers.

Capture the Momentum

John values his opening statements as perhaps the single most important moment in the trial. His goal is simple: present a memorable, thorough, intellectually robust, and emotionally powerful summary of the case. John hopes to *overwhelm* the jury with the totality of the evidence. He understands an important principle of jury trials: If you win the jury early, all you have to do is *keep* them. If you don't win them early, you're playing "catch up" for the rest of the trial. *Momentum* is important in opening statements. That's why John's openings are *powerful* and *memorable*.

If you're trying to reach a friend or family member as a Christian case maker, create some momentum. A friend of mine, Ryan Moore, told me about a conversation he had with an atheist at his university. This nonbeliever told Ryan he believed the existence of true evil demonstrated the *non*existence of an all-loving and all-knowing God. He challenged Ryan to provide him with a compelling piece of evidence *for* God's existence. Ryan knew he was about to give an "opening statement." After pausing for a moment, he offered *evil* as the best evidence for God's existence: "When you describe something as truly (transcendently) *evil*, you're unwittingly acknowledging the existence of a true, objective, transcendent standard of *good*. But if there isn't a transcendent, objectively good God to act as that standard, 'evil' is nothing more than a matter of your personal opinion. *True evil* requires *a true standard of good* by which to measure it. That's why evil is evidence *for* God's existence." Ryan made a memorable, intellectually robust, and emotionally powerful opening statement, and he made it in less than a minute. Ryan's opening started the conversation moving with *momentum*.

Don't underestimate the importance of a fast start, and remember, every conversation about Jesus starts long before you begin to make the case with words. You've got time to think about how you approach people, to develop the character required to gain their trust, and to practice what you have to say. Get ready *now*, so you can jump in eagerly and make a great opening statement.

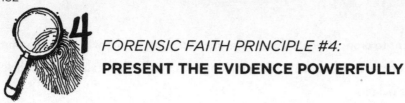

FORENSIC FAITH PRINCIPLE #4:
PRESENT THE EVIDENCE POWERFULLY

Once the opening statements are complete, it's time for each attorney to back up their claims with *evidence*. Attorneys understand that jurors aren't likely to trust their opening claims if these claims can't be supported evidentially. The "presentation of evidence" section of the trial provides each attorney with an opportunity to do just that.

Jesus also understood the expectations of His listeners. He knew they weren't likely to trust His claims if those claims couldn't be supported with evidence. That's one of the reasons why Jesus performed so many miracles. He told His listeners these miracles verified His claims of deity (John 10:25) and warned those who would not believe the evidence of the miracles (Luke 10:13–16). Along the way, He performed at least thirty-seven miracles; approximately twenty-two were recorded by Matthew, twenty by Mark, twenty-one by Luke, and eight by John, who said he recorded the miracles "so that you may believe that Jesus is the Christ, the Son of God; and that believing you may have life in His name" (John 20:31). Jesus was a masterful "evidence presenter."

Christian case makers also need to be ready to present the evidence for what they believe when making the case for Christianity. I've observed some excellent *criminal* "evidence presenters" over the years, and they all possessed similar attributes. If you are willing to adopt these simple principles, you'll improve your ability to present the evidence and make the case.

Be Self-Effacing and Gracious

The evidence-presentation portion of the trial is by far the longest. It might take weeks or months for both sides to present the evidence for their cases. During this extended period of time, the jury will have an opportunity to evaluate every aspect of the attorneys, including their *character*. For this reason, it is incredibly important to avoid arrogance. The most effective communicators are gracious, likeable, and unassuming. They poke fun at themselves, they don't take themselves too seriously, and they lower their guard when appropriate. They're *self-effacing*. In addition, they are gracious but tough. Jurors expect common courtesy to be extended to each witness, even when a witness is testifying against what the attorney claims is true. Each witness is to be treated with dignity unless they've perjured themselves by lying. Even when this happens, shrewd attorneys must maintain their character as they expose the motives of the lying witness. Character is important. Juries have been known to make a decision based on *how they feel about an attorney* rather than what *they think about the evidence*.

Your conversations about Christianity may also take an extended period of time. Some of my interactions with friends or family members have been going on for *years*. That's a long time for my "jury" to assess my character; I have to make sure my *evidential confidence* doesn't result in *obnoxious arrogance*. This is always a danger, especially when interacting with people online. The New Atheist movement is replete with aggressive ambassadors who are quick to lose their temper and happy to ridicule. It's tempting to "fight fire with fire" when interacting with some of these harsh critics of Christianity. Don't do it. Retain your sense of humor. Be gracious, even if you catch someone lying. Don't match arrogance with arrogance. Learn to take a punch and laugh it off. You'll be much more likeable and a much better communicator. You don't want your friends and family members to make a decision based on *how they feel about you* rather than what *they think about the evidence*.

Be Accessible

There are times when the technical aspects of a trial can be overwhelming to a jury. DNA experts, material experts, or behavioral psychologists aren't always gifted at communicating their expertise to laymen. It's the job of the attorneys to help these experts avoid esoteric, proprietary language. Attorneys have to help the experts translate their testimony so the jury can understand it. Accessibility is key. Good communicators "throw the ball so people can catch it" and avoid confusing, esoteric, technical jargon.

Christian case makers also need to be good translators. When researching and

Forensic Faith
Communication Guideline:
ELIMINATE YOUR "CHRISTIANESE"

I've given you some examples of words Christians sometimes use with one another that are confusing or offensive to nonbelievers. Over the next two or three weeks, start to sensitize yourself to your own collection of confusing "Christianese."

Listen to yourself, particularly when you're talking to other Christians. Make a list of all the words you need to translate, and write down some alternate, accessible variations. Then take the time to change the way you communicate, focusing less on those who already understand Christianity and more on those who don't.

writing *God's Crime Scene*, I quickly realized the challenge I was facing as a translator. How would I communicate incredibly complicated scientific and philosophical concepts without losing the audience I was hoping to reach? I knew I couldn't simply quote my sources verbatim. Instead, I needed to find a way to avoid mysterious, technical language and recommunicate their statements with accessible analogies and relatable stories. If you're trying to share the truth of Christianity with a friend or family member, you also need to avoid esoteric *Christian language*. Christians have their own set of proprietary terms that require translation. Here are just a few terms in need of translation:

"Be born again." This term is well-known but poorly understood by non-Christians. As an atheist, I wasn't sure what it meant to be "born again." Are "born again" Christians different from "regular" Christians? The term needs translating for those who are unfamiliar with the language. One possible translation might be "Reconsider your status before a perfect, holy God, accept the forgiveness offered by Jesus, and begin a new life as a Christian."

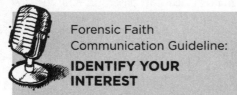

Forensic Faith
Communication Guideline:
**IDENTIFY YOUR
INTEREST**

We're all designed and wired differently, and God uses our collective gifts to accomplish His goals. Your interest is the key to successful communication. But first, you have to identify what you're passionate about.

I have a colleague who is a medical doctor. Once he became a Christian, he found himself making the case for the resurrection based on what he knew about death symptomology. He sifted through the passion accounts to find the evidence and typically finds himself making the case for the resurrection based on his medical expertise. What are you passionate about? How will your passions determine how you make the case for Christianity?

"You need to be repentant." As an atheist, I found this expression both archaic and offensive. It sounded like a word from the dark ages, and it insinuated that I was bad—long before I knew how bad I was. Here's a possible translation: "You and I might be 'good' at times, but we're not 'perfect.' If God is all-powerful, He has the ability to be perfect. The only way imperfect creatures like you and me can be united to a perfect God is to accept the pardon He's offering for our imperfection."

"Invite Jesus into your heart." This sounds confusing, sappy, and emotional. I know people invite girlfriends or boyfriends into their hearts, but what does that have to do with God? Here's a translation: "When we admit our imperfections, believe Jesus died on

the cross to pay the price for our moral failings, and accept His sacrifice, we can start a new relationship with God."

"Be washed by the blood of the Lamb." As a skeptical, unbelieving homicide detective, this expression conjured a number of images for me, but none of them had anything to do with God. Here's a helpful translation: "The death of one perfect man (Jesus) provides forgiveness for the rest of us."

"Be sanctified." "Sanctified" sounds an awful lot like "sanctimonious" to most people, and it's a word that's seldom used outside of Christian circles. This translation may start to move us in the right direction: "Grateful people are selfless people. Christians who understand how much they've been forgiven are changed over time."

Starting to get the idea? If you want your presentation to be accessible to your "jury," you need to become a good translator. Start "throwing the ball so people can catch it."

Be Strategic

Not all evidence is created equal. Attorneys must decide which evidences they will (or will not) present to the jury, and which witnesses they will (or will not) call to the witness stand. Not every piece of evidence or potential witness has the same importance to the case. Attorneys have to decide what they will highlight and what they will minimize. Are some of these evidences more confusing than they are persuasive? Are some more prejudicial than convincing? In a similar way, attorneys also have to decide which experts are necessary to make their case. Some cases require doctors, coroners, DNA experts, material evidence experts, or weapons specialists. Good communicators strategically limit the kinds of evidence they present and carefully select the experts they call.

When I first decided to accept my duty as a Christian case maker, I felt overwhelmed by all the diverse disciplines from which I could make the case for Christianity. I was already in my thirties and busier than ever as a homicide detective. I couldn't imagine how I would ever find the time to master all the philosophy and science. So I decided to *specialize*. I picked the one line of evidence that most interested me and spent as much time as possible learning everything I could. As a police officer, I resonated with the argument for God's existence from objective moral truths (commonly known as the Axiological Argument). Here is a good example of how this argument might be formulated:

1. If God did not exist, objective moral values would not exist.

2. Objective moral values do exist.

3. Therefore, God exists.[13]

As a relatively new believer, I focused on this argument when making the case for Christianity. It required me to study so I could defend the claims of the argument. Do objective moral laws really exist? Couldn't these objective values be the result of something *other* than God? I knew I needed to articulate the case and respond to objections. Having only one argument in my arsenal, my case wasn't as cumulative or broad as I would have liked, but it was a start. If you want to be a good communicator and don't know a lot about all the possible forms of evidence, strategically limit the kinds of evidence you present and carefully select the experts you call.

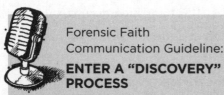

Forensic Faith
Communication Guideline:

ENTER A "DISCOVERY" PROCESS

If you want to know what the other side is going to say or do "at trial," you'll need some "discovery" of your own. Believe me, the other side has been listening to what Christians have been saying for some time now. Have you taken the time to listen to what *their* culture has to say?

A frustrated Christian friend recently told me he's so upset with the trajectory of the country and the increase of secularism that he feels like withdrawing altogether. If you also feel that way, let me encourage you. Now is *not* the time to retreat. Instead, it's the best time ever to gather "discovery" from the vocal opposition so you can be prepared. Read the papers, magazines, and websites that represent non-Christian views. Listen to what they're saying so you can anticipate the objectives and act preemptively.

Be a Good Questioner

When witnesses testify in a case, they do so in response to *questions*. The best prosecutors and defense attorneys are excellent questioners. In fact, if attorneys don't ask the right questions during direct and cross examination, jurors won't have the information they need to make a decision. Attorneys question witnesses in a very intentional way. First, they ask penetrating questions to understand what the witness is claiming and to expose any potential motives or biases. Next, they listen carefully for contradictions or inconsistencies. Finally, they point out the discrepancies in the testimony to either correct misunderstandings or highlight intentional misrepresentations. Good communicators ask good questions and allow the answers to chart their course.

If you want to be a good Christian case maker, you need to understand the value of good questions. No one understands this better than Greg Koukl (the friend I mentioned in the previous chapter). His book *Tactics: A Game Plan for Discussing Your Christian Convictions* is the finest instruction manual for good Christian conversations available today. Greg is a fan of Detective Columbo, the famous fictional detective popularized by actor Peter Falk in the 1970s. Columbo was consistently underestimated by the people he questioned, but he listened carefully to their responses and solved every case. In the spirit of Detective Columbo, Greg suggests all Christian case makers ask two important questions when someone makes a claim about Christianity or God: (1) What do you mean by that? and (2) Why do you think that's true? These two simple questions will help you clarify what people believe and why they believe it.

Listen carefully for the attributes of truth when people respond to these two questions. Truth isn't all that hard to recognize, and false ideas are even easier to identify. In *God's Crime Scene*, I describe three characteristics of errant case making. When attorneys find themselves trying to defend something untrue, they either (1) make a claim that isn't supported by the evidence, (2) errantly redefine key terms to conform to their argument, or (3) make claims that are logically inconsistent. Listen for these three characteristics when talking with your friends, and be ready to point out their errors with gentleness and respect.

In a recent conversation with a friend, for example, I used two "Columbo" questions to help her think through her position. My friend told me she had been "pro-choice" her entire adult life. I asked, "What do you mean by 'pro-choice'?" She told me she thought women should have the right to do what they want with their bodies, including the right to have an abortion. I asked another "what" question: "What, in your opinion, is the unborn?"

"Well," she said, "I don't think it's a person, if that's what you mean." I asked her a form of the second Columbo question: "Why do you believe that? Why don't you think the unborn are human persons?"

"Because they are not independent human beings. They're completely dependent on their mothers for survival." I had a choice at this point in the conversation. I recognized that she was errantly redefining human "personhood." I could have made a counter-claim of my own at this point or simply told her she was wrong. But I wanted to be gentle and respectful, so I used a few *questions* to point out the error in her thinking: "It sounds like you're saying physical independence and autonomy are the basis for human identity, am I hearing you correctly? But if that is true, does that mean *aging* or *injured* adults who are dependent on pace makers or dialysis machines would also have to be considered less human than others? Does one's level of dependency really determine one's personhood?" My goal was to help her see the error in her thinking in the least threatening way possible. Good questions can help accomplish this goal.

Be Preemptive

Prior to starting a trial, each side must release information to the other about the witnesses and evidence they'll call and present during the trial. This information exchange is called "discovery," and it's designed to prevent one side from "ambushing" the other when it's too late to obtain refuting evidence or too late to fashion a response. "Discovery" allows both sides to know the other's case *before* they begin. For this reason, good prosecutors think *preemptively* and do their homework about the opposition's case and the team they'll face in trial. The more they understand how the opponent thinks and behaves in trial, the better they'll be able to *anticipate* the objections and strategy the other side may pursue. Prosecutors often address the opposition's evidence (at least indirectly) even *before* the defense calls a witness, and they strategically plan for how they might respond to any objections offered. After reviewing the discovery and evaluating what they know about the defense team, good prosecutors act *preemptively* and *anticipate objections*.

Unfortunately, there isn't a formal "discovery" process for our spiritual conversations. If we want to know what our friends or family members are going to say in advance of our discussions, we had better take the time to love and know our hearers and prepare ourselves to answer each and every possible response they might offer. That's not an easy task to accomplish. But the more you read about the claims of atheism and the more time you take to understand your hearers, the better chance you'll have to act preemptively and anticipate objections. Are you reading what the opposition has to say about Christianity? Have you thought about how you might respond to the common objections offered by the culture? This may be the only "discovery" you get prior to talking with nonbelievers. How well do you know the people with whom you are sharing the truth? Have you been a good listener? Do you know why they might reject Christianity or have misgivings about Christians? Do you know if their objections are rational, emotional, or volitional? Take the time to review the "discovery" and evaluate what you know about your hearers so you can *act preemptively* and *anticipate objections.*

The presentation of evidence is the "nuts and bolts" part of any jury trial. Attorneys make a persuasive opening statement and then spend the majority of the trial making good on their evidential promises by providing the evidence they previewed for the jury. Once this is done, each side has one last opportunity to convince the jury. It doesn't come in the form of a *statement*, however. Instead, it is delivered in the form of an *argument*.

FORENSIC FAITH PRINCIPLE #5:
MAKE A CLOSING ARGUMENT PERSUASIVELY

Before the attorneys release the jury to deliberate on what they've seen or heard, they make one final effort to convince the jury of their position. Opening statements are relatively straightforward previews of the case to come; closing arguments are impassioned pleas for the jury to remember what they've seen and to make the right decision.

Unsurprisingly, Jesus was an amazing "closer." After His most famous message, the Sermon on the Mount, Jesus had an opportunity to leave His listeners with something powerful as He summarized the importance of the words He had just spoken. Here's what He said:

> Therefore everyone who hears these words of Mine and acts on them, may be compared to a wise man who built his house on the rock. And the rain fell, and the floods came, and the winds blew and slammed against that house; and yet it did not fall, for it had been founded on the rock. Everyone who hears these words of Mine and does not act on them, will be like a foolish man who built his house on the sand. The rain fell, and the floods came, and the winds blew and slammed against that house; and it fell—and great was its fall. (Matthew 7:24–27)

The crowds were blown away. Jesus taught with confident authority, referenced the importance of the sermon He had just given, and called His audience to act on His words. Jesus understood the value of a good "closing argument."

Every good courtroom movie includes a dramatic closing argument. I was asked to play a small role in *God's Not Dead 2*, where I appeared in a courtroom scene as an expert witness (I testified on the reliability of the New Testament Gospels). The fictional attorneys in this movie, Prosecutor Tom Endler and Defense Attorney Pete Kane, continue the dramatic tradition of courtroom movies by offering emotional, entertaining closing arguments of their own. While real criminal attorneys aren't always as theatrical as their cinematic counterparts, we can learn a lot from the way they present closing arguments. Much of what we learn can be applied to our duty as Christian case makers.

Close Confidently

Good communicators close their argument with confidence. After we successfully investigated and prosecuted Douglas Bradford (the defendant I described in the previous chapter), John Lewin was asked a question during the *Dateline* taping. Bradford had hired Robert Shapiro (the famed defense attorney who first represented O. J. Simpson) as his defense attorney. After the trial was over, Keith Morrison asked John if he was intimidated by having to face Shapiro. John responded succinctly by telling Keith that he was confident because he had an advantage over Shapiro: John's position was *true*. John's *confidence* was rooted in his *evidential certainty*, and it's a lot easier to remain calm when you are certain.

Christian case makers ought to reflect a similar certainty. We have the truth. If we're familiar with the evidence supporting our case, we ought to allow our *certainty* to result in *confidence*. If you've ever owned a dog and visited a dog park, you know the difference between Great Danes and Chihuahuas. Danes walk quietly with confidence. They don't have anything to prove; they are, after all, the biggest dogs in the yard. Chihuahuas, on the other hand, are the loudest dogs in the park, and you know why: they're typically the smallest dog around. If, as Christians, we have the truth, our worldview is the "big dog" among worldviews. There's no reason to panic, no reason to "puff up," no reason to make a lot of unnecessary noise. Our closing argument should be made *confidently*, based on our evidential certainty.

Summarize Visually

Every closing argument must summarize the evidence that was presented in trial, and it's true that a picture is worth a thousand words. When used as part of your closing summary, visual tools help jurors remember the facts, connect the dots, understand the depth and power of the case, and make a reasonable inference. We typically employ images as part of our closing arguments. In *Cold-Case Christianity*, I provided an example of what a cumulative case might look like when presented *visually*. Do you remember the case against the man who was accused of bludgeoning his girlfriend in the previous chapter? Go back and take a look at the diagram we used to highlight the cumulative nature of the case. Although you may not be a trained illustrator, I bet you could create an adequate "napkin version" of this diagram to help someone understand the strength of the evidence:

The cumulative case is more obvious when illustrated in this way rather than by simply offering the evidence in list form.

As a Christian case maker, I still rely on images and diagrams to make my case. If I am presenting the case for Christianity to a class or large audience, I project my diagrams and visual images on a screen. If I am talking with a friend in a more intimate setting, I inevitably pull out a napkin or piece of paper to start visualizing the case. Here, for example, is a diagram from *Cold-Case Christianity* illustrating the cumulative case for Peter as the source of Mark's gospel:

The following diagram (from *God's Crime Scene*) illustrates seven factors we must consider when trying to understand why God might allow any act of evil:

In each of these examples, complicated concepts are visualized in an effort to make the evidence (and the arguments) clearer and more compelling.

Offer a "Rebuttal" (with Gentleness and Respect)

After the closing arguments, the prosecution has an additional (and final) opportunity to address the jury in his or her *rebuttal*. In jury trials, the prosecution gets the final word because it has the burden of proof. In this last argument before the jury, the prosecution focuses in more narrowly on the defense attorney's closing argument in an effort to point out weaknesses or logical inconsistencies. Prosecutors must be courageous in their rebuttals and squarely address the deficiencies they see in the opposition's case while carefully retaining an inoffensive character that won't alienate the jury. This delicate balance between spirited confrontation and professional character is sometimes difficult to gauge and maintain, but it's important. This is the last chance the attorney has to convince the jury of both the strength of the prosecution's case and the weakness of the defense's response. Prosecutors typically treat this final argument as a "now or never" moment. Their goal is simple: address the weaknesses in the opposition's case and leave the jury with something powerful to think about.

Many of my Christian friends are uncomfortable "rebutting" the claims made by unbelieving friends, coworkers, and family members because they don't want to be seen as *judgmental*. In fact, some Christians think we've actually been *commanded* to be *non*confrontational and *non*judgmental. They typically cite Jesus's words in the Sermon on the Mount:

> Forensic Faith
> Communication Guideline:
> **BE CREATIVE**
>
> Now that you've seen a few examples of how you might illustrate the truth claims of Christianity, take a minute to be creative. You don't have to be an artist to illustrate a Christian concept.
>
> Practice your diagramming skills with the following assignment: try to think of a way to illustrate the triune nature of God. You can either illustrate a metaphor you've heard from a pastor or teacher, or you can try to create your own diagram depicting the three members of the Godhead. Do your best to create a diagram that maintains the essential aspects of God's nature (God exists in three persons, each person is divine, yet there is only one God). Your diagram doesn't have to be elaborate. After making an attempt, conduct an image search online for "Christian trinity diagram." You'll find dozens of examples to compare with your own.

Matthew 7:1

Do not judge so that you will not be judged.

This statement seems direct and unambiguous, doesn't it? But remember our principle from the last chapter: we shouldn't *read just one verse of the Bible in isolation*. So let's take a look at Jesus's words about judgment in their proper context:

Matthew 7:1–5

Do not judge so that you will not be judged. For in the way you judge, you will be judged; and by your standard of measure, it will be measured to you. Why do you look at the speck that is in your brother's eye, but do not notice the log that is in your own eye? Or how can you say to your brother, "Let me take the speck out of your eye," and behold, the log is in your own eye? You hypocrite, first take the log out of your own eye, and then you will see clearly to take the speck out of your brother's eye.

Jesus isn't telling us we should never judge but that we should never judge *hypocritically*. If we point out the error in our brother's life yet possess that *same* error in our own, the "standard of measure" we use to judge our brother could certainly be used to judge us as well. That's why Jesus refers to someone like this as a "hypocrite" and tells us to "*first* take the log out of your own eye, and *then* you will see clearly to take the speck out of your brother's eye." We are *called* to point out error in others ("take the speck out of your brother's eye"), but *only after* making sure we aren't guilty of the same error ("first take the log out of your own eye").

Showing people the weaknesses or logical inconsistencies in their worldview is an important part of Christian case making, but be certain you've thought through your own position and haven't presented it in a

Forensic Faith Challenge:
CHRISTIANS ARE INTOLERANT

Christians are often called intolerant, especially when we *disagree* with moral values and ideas held by non-Christians in our culture. Voltaire once wrote: "Of all religions the Christian is without doubt the one which should inspire tolerance most, although up to now the Christians have been the most intolerant of all men."[14] How might you help people understand the difference between disagreeing and being intolerant? What might you say to help people understand the nature of true tolerance?

For a suggested response and resources to help you answer similar objections, see the Rebuttal Notes section.

way that is logically inconsistent or factually untrue. Take the "log" out of your own case before you take the "speck" out of your brother's case.

In every conversation I have about the case for Christianity, I hope to leave people with something insightful and illuminating, just like a good prosecutor. Although I don't expect to have the last word in these conversations, I do hope to make the *last* memorable statement. If a claim has been offered or an objection has been raised against Christianity, I do my best to offer a gracious rebuttal, seeking a Christlike balance between true tolerance and nonhypocritical judgment. My goal is simple: address the weaknesses in opposing views and leave people with something powerful to think about.

Ask for a Decision Passionately

Passion is incredibly important in criminal case making. If jurors don't sense urgency and passion on the part of the prosecutor, they're not likely to feel a sense of urgency or passion themselves. If the attorneys aren't excited about their cases, why should they expect the jury to be? Prosecutors and defense attorneys possess more than just passion; they have *directed passion*. They want their impassioned efforts to result in *a decision*. For this reason, they end their final arguments by asking specifically for the jury to decide in their favor. In fact, they typically remind the jury of the importance of their duty as jurors and the critical nature of the decision they are about to make. When jurors understand what's at stake and are enthusiastically engaged in the arguments, they are far more likely to come to a decision and come to it quickly.

Spiritual decisions are even *more* critical than jury decisions because there's so much more at stake. A jury decision dictates a defendant's *temporal* future, but spiritual decisions dictate a person's *eternal* future. Given the importance of spiritual decisions, shouldn't we, as Christian case makers, be passionate and goal directed? I'm always surprised when I hear someone tell me how they were led to Christ by someone who was just courageous enough to ask them for a decision. The best evangelists I know are fearless. They are passionate and unafraid, and they never forget to ask someone if they are ready to change their mind and become a follower of Christ.

I recognize that it's not always appropriate or possible to offer the gospel or lead someone in a prayer of salvation. And as a new Christian case maker, you may not yet feel confident or courageous enough to ask for the most important decision a person could make. But it's *always* possible to leave people with something powerful to think about and challenge them to consider seriously what you've just offered. If you're not yet comfortable to ask for a decision for Christ, at least ask for a decision to *think*. Remind the people you care about of the importance of the topic at hand and the critical nature of the evidence you've presented. If you can help them understand what's at stake, and can engage them passionately in the arguments, they are far more likely to come to a decision and come to it quickly.

Place the Case in the Hands of the Jury Confidently

Once the presentations are complete, attorneys place the case in the hands of the jury. As I described in the beginning of this chapter, this is sometimes hard to do. The prosecutor and defense attorney have to trust that they've done all they could do. Now it's time for the jury to do *their* job. One way to weather the inevitable anxiety that often occurs while everyone is waiting for a decision is to simply remember the *team effort* required to successfully prosecute or represent a defendant. No single attorney usually makes the case alone; instead, they rely on the help of investigators, paralegal assistants, support staff, and interns. It's a team effort, so the success (or failure) really isn't resting on any one person in the process. While this truth isn't always completely comforting, it is helpful to remember when a decision is hanging in the balance.

I'm sometimes tempted to see my spiritual conversations as a solo effort. While I recognize the sovereignty of God in calling His children to Himself, I often struggle to find my own role in evangelism. Like a game of tennis, I occasionally feel like I'm all alone, volleying back and forth with a friend who's a better athlete. We're at the French Open, playing on clay. It's hot and the stakes are high, and the entire world is watching on ESPN. Whatever I do (or don't do) and whatever I say (or don't say) will make all the difference. Every shot I miss is my fault; there's no one else to blame. But this analogy doesn't actually apply to my efforts as a Christian case maker. Evangelism is more like a game of *baseball*. It's a *team effort*. In every conversation I have with unbelieving friends, I am mindful of the value of *singles*. I can't "win" every encounter, and it's unreasonable to expect to hit a home run every time I step up to the plate. If I get the right pitch, I'll swing, and if I get on base, great. Singles are important in baseball games because my teammates can turn my single into a winning run.

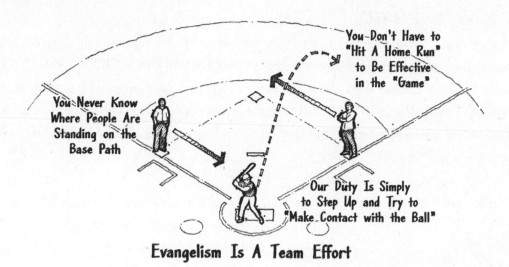

Evangelism Is A Team Effort

Every story of conversion typically involves *incremental* decision making. People rarely make dramatic shifts in their thinking overnight. Instead, they usually move around the bases one base at a time as they consider the truth claims of Christianity and respond to the events in their lives. They may stand on second or third base for an extended period of time before advancing, and you never know where they may be on the base path when you engage them as a case maker. This was my personal experience as someone considering the claims of Christianity. I spent some time "running the bases"; it took a while for me to process and consider the evidence. If you had approached me while I was engaged in this process, you might not have known precisely where I was along the base path. In fact, you might have gotten frustrated with me when I didn't respond favorably (or immediately) to your efforts to share the truth. But I was listening all along, inching closer to home plate.

Maybe that's why I'm eager to talk to people and help them overcome an objection or advance their understanding just a "base" or two. I remember my own process as a base runner, and I know this isn't a game of tennis. I'm part of a team sport and just one in a *series* of batters trying to move my seeking friends along the base path. I step up to the plate, try to get a sense of what the pitcher is throwing, and do my best to make an appropriate decision on how to respond. On rare occasions, I may swing for the fences, but sometimes the wiser choice is simply to make contact with the ball, get on base if possible, or take a "walk" if the pitcher is throwing wildly. It's not all on me. I don't have to win the game all by myself.

GROW, THEN GO

I'll never forget the first time we received a guilty verdict in a high-profile cold case. The local Fox News reporters were waiting on the steps of the court building. It felt like a scene from a movie. Cameramen were everywhere, and the reporters were eager to get an interview. In the midst of all the post-trial chaos, I looked for the family of the victim. I watched them as they answered the reporters' questions and held back tears of joy and relief. I suddenly realized why I was working these cases.

I was working for the families.

Each time we successfully made the case in front of a jury, we helped a family find justice. "Closure" as we like to think of it, was usually elusive. But justice was often enough to transform people forever. With every new case, our team grew in its ability to effectively investigate and communicate the truth, and with every new case, we were only more committed to *doing it again*. We learned an important principle: the more you *grow* as a case maker, the more you want to *go* make the case.

Jesus understood this principle. He left His disciples with an important task. They had matured and *grown* spiritually in the years since first meeting Him. Now it was time to *go* make disciples:

Matthew 28:18–20 (ESV)

And Jesus came and said to them, "All authority in heaven and on earth has been given to me. Go therefore and make disciples of all nations, baptizing them in the name of the Father and of the Son and of the Holy Spirit,

Forensic Faith Assignment:
START MAKING THE CASE

The best way to *learn* something is to force yourself to teach it to others. When you know you have to communicate something publicly, you're far more likely to be motivated to learn it yourself.

You might not think you know enough to make the case to others, but regardless of who you are, there's *someone* in your world who knows less and needs your help. If you're willing to create a teaching opportunity for yourself, you'll accelerate your progress as a Christian case maker dramatically. Pick a friend or loved one you'd like to talk to, volunteer to teach a session at your local church, start a blog, or write a social media post.

You can talk about becoming a Christian case maker until you're blue in the face, but it's just talk until you actually step out and get started. It's your duty and you know enough now about how to proceed. Get started.

teaching them to observe all that I have commanded you. And behold, I am
with you always, to the end of the age."

Jesus told the disciples to go make *more* disciples. Grow disciples, then go do it again. Jesus
wanted His apostles to teach *others* to do what He had already taught *them*. That's why *their*
great commission is now *our* great commission.

If we want to observe all that Jesus commanded, we need to take an approach similar to
the one Jesus taught the apostles. As contemporary Christian case makers, we should follow
the instruction of our Master:

> **Luke 24:46–49** (ESV)
> Thus it is written, that the Christ should suffer and on the third day rise from
> the dead, and that repentance for the forgiveness of sins should be proclaimed
> in his name to all nations, beginning from Jerusalem. You are witnesses of
> these things. And behold, I am sending the promise of my Father upon you.

> **Acts 1:8** (ESV)
> But you will receive power when the Holy Spirit has come upon you, and
> you will be my witnesses in Jerusalem and in all Judea and Samaria, and to
> the end of the earth.

By the power of the Holy Spirit, the first Christians shared the direct evidence of their
eyewitness observations. Making *disciples* involved making the *case*. It's not any different today.

You may not presently be the kind of case maker you'd like to be. Don't be discouraged;
the disciples weren't the kind of case makers they wanted to be when they first met Jesus. It
took them three years, hundreds of life experiences, and thousands of hours sitting at the feet
of the Master. It takes *time* to become a good case maker. How often did Peter falter before
he boldly made the case at Pentecost? Think about Simon Peter in the opening chapters of
the Gospels; could you ever imagine he would become the confident leader we see in the
book of Acts? It didn't happen overnight. He struggled, made mistakes, learned from his
errors, and took incremental steps toward becoming a great Christian case maker.

Now it's your turn. Don't be afraid to struggle, make mistakes, learn from your errors, and take incremental steps toward becoming the best Christian case maker you can be.

As you *grow* as a case maker, you'll want to *go* make disciples. There's nothing more satisfying than partnering with the Holy Spirit to make the case for Christianity. As a criminal case maker, I work for families because I want to see God's work of transformation, and I want to be a small part of the process. As a Christian case maker, I work for our Christian family for the very same reason. Join me. Become a Christian case maker, and watch God transform the hearts and minds of unbelievers, even as He transforms the nature of our Christian family.

BECOME A SHEEPDOG

Wendy Hoynes looked happier than I had ever seen her before. In fact, standing next to the man she was about to marry, I hardly recognized her. The broken, distraught woman I knew just three years prior had been *transformed*. When I met her, Wendy could barely speak for thirty minutes without crying. Her life had been derailed at an early age, and she hadn't allowed herself to blossom or move through the sorrow she had been experiencing for many years.

Today she was a new woman. Dressed in white, beaming and expectant, she was ready to take on the future with hope and confidence. Her life had been transformed by God, and He did it with a bit of case making.

Wendy's sister, Robin, had been murdered in our city in the 1980s. When it happened, Wendy was a young teenager. The murder shocked our community and changed the trajectory of Wendy's life. Robin was the most committed Christian Wendy knew, and her death caused Wendy to question God and the meaning of her own life. When I first told Wendy I was taking over the case, nearly twenty-five years after the murder, she immediately burst into tears. Grateful but cautious, Wendy couldn't imagine her life without the pain and uncertainty of her sister's unsolved murder.

When the crime occurred, it paralyzed Wendy's entire family. Her parents never fully recovered, and her father died before we were able to arrest and convict the murderer. When the guilty verdict was finally delivered, the lives of those who survived were changed forever. They had been released from the uncertainty and injustice of the crime. While they didn't experience "closure" (few people really do), they did see justice served. As a result, they began to do things they hadn't done in years, and they celebrated holidays they had previously placed "on hold." Life started anew as the result of the case-making efforts of the prosecution team.

Of all the cases I've worked in my career, this one was perhaps the most gratifying. I watched God work in the midst of terrible evil, and I was grateful to play a small role in Wendy's story of transformation. Her case reminded me of the importance of my role as a case maker and renewed my desire to help others experience the same kind of transformation.

THE IMPORTANCE OF SHEEPDOGS

Law enforcement officers (like military personnel) view the world through a unique lens. We tend to see people in one of two distinct categories: as "sheep" or "wolves." Jesus also recognized this distinction. He often referred to His followers as "sheep." When Jesus was saddened to see His people disheartened, Matthew described it in the following way: "He felt compassion for them, because they were distressed and dispirited like *sheep* without a shepherd" (Matthew 9:36). Those who hadn't yet trusted Jesus were also described similarly: Jesus said He "was sent only to the lost *sheep* of the house of Israel" (Matthew 15:24). When I first read these "sheep" passages, I was encouraged and inspired. In many ways, Jesus seemed to be talking like a *police officer*. When commissioning His disciples to preach in neighboring communities, He even told them, "Behold, I send you out as sheep in the midst of wolves" (Matthew 10:16).

After working cases like Wendy's, I understand how dangerous life can be. The world is filled with potential victims ("sheep") and perilous victimizers ("wolves"). Police officers stand in the gap; we're the thin blue line separating the sheep from the wolves. We are *sheepdogs*.

Even in Jesus's day, sheepdogs played an important role in the shepherd's pasture. If you've ever worked with sheep, you know they aren't the smartest animals in the field. Sheep are typically unable to defend themselves from predators, and they aren't clever enough to understand their vulnerabilities. Sheep don't know they have a *need* for protection; they are unaware of danger until it is too late.

Sheepdogs *do* understand the danger, and they're better equipped to meet the challenges. In spite of the value sheepdogs provide to the flock, however, sheep are sometimes hesitant about them. In fact, most sheep find sheepdogs *annoying*; they're always nipping at their hooves and trying to herd them in one direction or another. But one thing is certain: *If the yard was filled with sheepdogs, there wouldn't be a wolf problem.*

Christian case makers are also sheepdogs. It's our duty to protect the sheep from the wolves who seek to draw the sheep away from the Shepherd. The sheep are often unprepared to face the challenges presented by the culture (and equally unaware of the dangers). They sometimes view sheepdogs with hesitation; Christian "apologists" are much less popular than other speakers in the church. But *if the church was filled with sheepdogs, there would be little or no threat from wolves at all.*

If the Church was filled with sheepdogs,
there would be little or no threat from wolves at all

That's why it's so important for those of us who already understand our duty as Christian case makers to help others see *their* duty as well. Time is short, and while there are certainly many incredibly valuable apologists in the Christian community, we can't wait for another "Million Dollar" apologist to rise up and protect us. Instead, we need a million "One Dollar" apologists. You may not feel like you're the biggest (or strongest) sheepdog in the field, but if *everyone* in your midst was a sheepdog of one kind or another, you would be in a safe place nonetheless. It's our duty, as Christians, to become sheepdogs and help the *rest of the sheep* see their duty as well.

So, what kind of sheepdog will you become? Wendy experienced the transformational power of criminal case making. It changed the trajectory of her *temporal life* and restored her confidence in the God who offers her *eternal life*. Christian case making is even *more* transformational. If you're willing to accept and embrace your Christian duty as a case maker, you'll change the trajectory of the lives around you, and you'll grow in confidence as a follower of Jesus.

This book (like my others) is a *gateway* book. It's not intended to be read at the *end* of a journey, but at the *beginning*. I hope it will ignite in you a desire to change the way you *think* about Christianity so you can change the way you *live* as a Christian. I hope it starts an investigative journey that will last a lifetime and that will encourage you to love Jesus with your mind as well as your heart and soul. Let's get busy *together* as the church. Now more than ever, it's time for us to accept our duty as case makers and start training. It's time to investigate the case for Christianity and communicate it convincingly to others. It's time for all of us to become sheepdogs. Now more than ever, we need to embrace a *forensic faith*.

BRIEF ANSWERS TO COMMON CHALLENGES

Here are some brief answers to the challenges offered in
the preceding four chapters. Pay attention to the way the
responses have been framed using some of the strategies
and principles we've described in *Forensic Faith*.

FORENSIC FAITH CHALLENGE #1: FAITH IS INCOMPATIBLE WITH REASON

Skeptics in our culture often argue faith is the opposite of reason. They also typically characterize themselves as the only "reasonable" people in the debate. How would you respond to this
common objection given what you now know about the evidential nature of Christianity? Can
you think of two or three things you might say to someone who makes this kind of claim? Here
is one way to respond:

Although there may be some unreasonable Christians, Jesus never asked us to abandon
reason as believers. In fact, the New Testament repeatedly tells us to use reason to determine if
Christianity is true. Consider these three points:

We're told not to be "like unreasoning animals" (Jude 4, 10), and we're told
to love God with our "mind" (Matthew 22:37–38).

Jesus told us to examine the evidence He provided (John 10:37–38), and
He stayed with His followers after the resurrection to provide them with
additional evidence (Acts 1:2–3).

Jesus's followers regularly "reasoned" with people to convince them Christianity is true (Acts 17:2–3), and we're told to "examine everything" carefully (1 Thessalonians 5:19–21).

So while not every Christian you meet may be able to defend what they believe with reason, the Christian worldview can be defended reasonably. I'd invite you to examine the evidence.

FORENSIC FAITH CHALLENGE #2: CHRISTIANS ARE HYPOCRITES

The hypocrisy of Christian believers is often cited by nonbelievers. One popular Internet meme declares, "I've got nothing against God: it's His fan club I can't stand." Author Brennan Manning (himself a believer) once put it this way: "The greatest single cause of atheism in the world today is Christians: who acknowledge Jesus with their lips, walk out the door, and deny Him by their lifestyle. That is what an unbelieving world simply finds unbelievable." How would you respond to this common objection? Below is one example of a reasonable response:

Everyone has an area of their lives where their beliefs are in contradiction with their actions. Hypocrisy describes something more than *occasional* misbehavior. When someone claims to believe one thing, but *continually* and *unapologetically* practices another, they can accurately be described as hypocritical. Given this is the true definition, much can be said about the nature of "Christian hypocrisy":

> True Christ followers are not hypocrites. Christians may fail on occasion, but if they *continually* and *unapologetically* deny the teaching of Jesus, they aren't really Christ followers, no matter what they may call themselves.

> True Christ followers are, however, imperfect. We still fail and struggle to change our behavior. Be patient with us; we're just like everyone else.

> True Christ followers are more likely to be called out for our misbehavior. After all, it's a lot easier to condemn the actions of those of us who are known to hold

to an exceedingly high standard than it is to judge people who are quiet about what they believe and can later nuance their values to match their behavior.

There are millions of Christians who strive daily to be more like Jesus. We will fail on occasion, but this does not mean we are hypocrites.

FORENSIC FAITH CHALLENGE #3: SCIENCE AND RELIGION ARE INCOMPATIBLE

Ernst Haeckel, the famous German naturalist biologist, once wrote, "Where faith commences, science ends." Ever heard someone say something similar when they argue science is incompatible with your Christian beliefs? Have you ever been told, as a Christian, that your beliefs contradict what we know is true scientifically? How would you respond to this common objection about the relationship between Christianity and science? Can you think of two or three things you might say to someone who makes this kind of claim? Here's one option:

Scientists study the "effects" they observe in the universe and then try to determine the most reasonable cause. If the evidence is best explained by the existence of a timeless, non-material, non-spatial personal Being, science may actually *confirm* the existence of God. But in order to evaluate the scientific evidence properly, you have to keep three things in mind:

Science doesn't "say" anything. Instead, scientists do. If the scientists evaluating the evidence reject the existence of God before they start, they will never interpret the evidence fairly, even if the evidence points to God as the best explanation.

An over-reliance on science is self-defeating. When people say, "Science is the only way to know the truth," they are making a *philosophical* (rather than *scientific*) claim that cannot be tested or discovered with science.

Many of the world's greatest scientists have believed in the existence of God, including historic thinkers like Johannes Kepler, Blaise Pascal, Isaac Newton, and Max Planck, and current scientists like John Polkinghorne, Francis Collins, Simon C. Morris, and Michael Behe.

The discoveries made by these great thinkers weren't inhibited by their belief in God. Instead, their theistic beliefs encouraged them to discover the immutable laws governing the universe.

FORENSIC FAITH CHALLENGE #4: CHRISTIANS ARE INTOLERANT

Christians are often called intolerant, especially when we disagree with moral values and ideas held by non-Christians in our culture. Voltaire once wrote: "Of all religions the Christian is without doubt the one which should inspire tolerance most, although up to now the Christians have been the most intolerant of all men." How might you help people understand the difference between disagreeing and being intolerant? What might you say to help people understand the nature of true tolerance? Here is a reasonable response:

Our culture has confused *agreement* with *tolerance*. Tolerance, as it is described popularly, is the notion that all views have equal merit and none should be considered any better than any other. If this definition is true, it's not surprising that Christians would be labeled intolerant when they don't agree with something accepted by the culture. But true, classic tolerance actually requires the following:

> A true definition: The classic definition of tolerance is much more akin to a "fair, objective, and permissive attitude towards those whose opinions, practices, race, religion, nationality etc. differ from one's own."[1]

> A thoughtful disagreement: Based on this definition, in order for two people to tolerate each other, they must maintain their disagreement. If they agree, there's no need for tolerance.

> A tactful demeanor: Even though I may hate a bad idea, as a Christian, I'm called to love the person who may hold the bad idea. In fact, I am called to love the people with whom I disagree.

True Christian believers follow the teaching of Jesus. We may disagree with you, but that alone doesn't make us intolerant.

RESOURCES TO HELP YOU BECOME A BETTER CASE MAKER

The following resources offer the evidence from a Christian perspective. These are popular-level publications and a great place to start. For an additional list of books, including more thorough publications and authors who write from an atheist perspective, please refer to the additional resources listed in *Cold-Case Christianity* and *God's Crime Scene*.

BOOKS TO HELP YOU INVESTIGATE THE EVIDENCE FOR THE EXISTENCE OF GOD

The Case for a Creator: A Journalist Investigates Scientific Evidence That Points toward God
by Lee Strobel (Zondervan, 2016)

God's Crime Scene: A Cold-Case Detective Examines the Evidence for a Divinely Created Universe
by J. Warner Wallace (David C Cook, 2015)

God's Not Dead: Evidence for God in an Age of Uncertainty
by Rice Broocks (Thomas Nelson, 2015)

God's Undertaker: Has Science Buried God?
by John C. Lennox (Lion Hudson, 2009)

I Don't Have Enough Faith to Be an Atheist
by Norman L. Geisler and Frank Turek (Crossway, 2004)

BOOKS TO HELP YOU INVESTIGATE THE EVIDENCE FOR CHRISTIANITY

The Case for Christ: A Journalist's Personal Investigation of the Evidence for Jesus
by Lee Strobel (Zondervan, 1998)

The Case for the Resurrection of Jesus
by Gary Habermas and Michael Licona (Kregel, 2004)

Cold-Case Christianity: A Homicide Detective Investigates the Claims of the Gospels
by J. Warner Wallace (David C Cook, 2013)

Confident Faith: Building a Firm Foundation for Your Beliefs
by Mark Mittelberg (Tyndale, 2013)

Mere Christianity
by C. S. Lewis (HarperOne, 2015)

The New Testament Documents: Are They Reliable?
by F. F. Bruce (Wm. B. Eerdmans, 2013)

BOOKS TO HELP YOU BECOME A BETTER CHRISTIAN COMMUNICATOR

A Reasonable Response: Answers to Tough Questions on God, Christianity, and the Bible
by William Lane Craig and Joseph E. Gorra (Moody, 2013)

Conversational Evangelism: How to Listen and Speak So You Can Be Heard
by David Geisler and Norman Geisler (Harvest, 2009)

How to Talk to a Skeptic: An Easy-to-Follow Guide for Natural Conversations and Effective Apologetics
by Donald J. Johnson (Bethany, 2013)

Tactics: A Game Plan for Discussing Your Christian Convictions
by Gregory Koukl (Zondervan, 2009)

Unsilenced: How to Voice the Gospel
by James Boccardo (WestBow, 2015)

BOOKS MAKING THE CASE FOR CHRISTIANITY FROM THE PERSPECTIVE OF A PROSECUTOR

Jesus on Trial: A Lawyer Affirms the Truth of the Gospels
by David Limbaugh (Regnery, 2014)

Christianity on Trial: A Lawyer Examines the Christian Faith
by W. Mark Lanier (InterVarsity, 2014)

Faith on Trial: Analyze the Evidence for the Death and Resurrection of Jesus
by Pamela Binnings Ewen (B&H, 2013)

The Testimony of the Evangelists: The Gospels Examined by the Rules of Evidence
by Simon Greenleaf (Kregel Classics, 1995)

BOOKS TO HELP YOU EXAMINE ALLEGED BIBLE "DIFFICULTIES"

The Big Book of Bible Difficulties: Clear and Concise Answers from Genesis to Revelation
by Norman Geisler and Thomas Howe (Baker Books, 2008)

Hard Sayings of the Bible
by Walter C. Kaiser Jr., Peter H. Davids, F. F. Bruce, and Manfred Brauch (IVP Academic, 1996)

Is God a Moral Monster?: Making Sense of the Old Testament God
by Paul Copan (Baker Books, 2011)

New International Encyclopedia of Bible Difficulties
by Gleason L. Archer Jr. (Zondervan, 2001)

RESOURCES TO HELP YOU ANSWER ATHEIST OBJECTIONS

10 Answers for Atheists: How to Have an Intelligent Discussion about the Existence of God
by Alex McFarland (Bethany, 2012)

Answering the Objections of Atheists, Agnostics, and Skeptics
by Ron Rhodes (Harvest, 2006)

Is God Just a Human Invention? And Seventeen Other Questions Raised by the New Atheists
by Sean McDowell and Jonathan Morrow (Kregel, 2010)

Stealing from God: Why Atheists Need God to Make Their Case
by Frank Turek (NavPress, 2015)

INTERNET RESOURCES TO HELP YOU STUDY THE BIBLE

Bible Gateway
www.biblegateway.com

Bible Hub
www.biblehub.com

BibleStudyTools.com
www.biblestudytools.com

INTERNET MINISTRIES TO HELP YOU GROW AS A CHRISTIAN CASE MAKER

Christian Research Institute
www.equip.org

Cold-Case Christianity with J. Warner Wallace
www.coldcasechristianity.com

Cross Examined with Frank Turek
www.crossexamined.org

Ravi Zacharias International Ministries
www.rzim.org

Reasonable Faith with William Lane Craig
www.reasonablefaith.org

Reasons to Believe
www.reasons.org

Stand to Reason
www.str.org

AN EXAMPLE OF A SPIRITUAL SURVEY TO HELP START A CONVERSATION

This survey was first developed by Brett Kunkle from Stand to Reason. Contact Brett at www.str.org if you would like more information about one of his Utah or university missions trips. Remember, the goal of a survey like this is not to get all the questions answered but to use the questions as a springboard for deeper conversations.

Do you believe in a supreme being or higher power?

Why or why not?
What do you think he, she, or it is like and why?

Do you believe truth exists? If so, do you think we can know truth?

Is there such thing as objective/absolute truth?
Is there religious truth? If so, how do we find it?

Do you believe there are moral facts (right and wrong) that everyone should follow? Or do you believe that morality is relative to individuals or cultures?

Why or why not?

Do you think abortion should be legal or illegal?

Why or why not?

Do you believe in an afterlife?

Why or why not?
If yes, what do you think the afterlife is like?

Who do you believe Jesus was?

Why do you believe this about Jesus?
Where do you get most of your information about Jesus?

What do you think about Christianity?

Why do you believe this?
What has given you this impression?

NOTES AND REFERENCES

PREFACE: TO PROTECT AND TO SERVE

1. For more information about the steady decline of those who identify themselves as Christians, refer to the ongoing research of the Pew Research Center, most recently, their study entitled "America's Changing Religious Landscape" (May 12, 2015, www.pewforum.org/2015/05/12/americas-changing-religious-landscape/).

2. C. S. Lewis, "Learning in War-Time," in *The Weight of Glory* (New York: HarperCollins, 2001), 58.

3. Surveys continue to demonstrate the disproportionate rate at which young people are walking away from the church. For more information on this disturbing trend, refer to the following resources:

Related to the Inability of Young Christians to Articulate Their Faith:

Christian Smith and Melinda Lundquist Denton, *Soul Searching: The Religious and Spiritual Lives of American Teenagers* (Oxford University Press, 2005).

Steve Wright, *reThink* (InQuest Ministries, 2007).

Josh McDowell and David Bellis, *The Last Christian Generation* (Green Key Books, 2006).

Related to the Departure of Young People from the Church:

T. C. Pinkney, "Remarks to the Southern Baptist Convention Executive Committee," Southern Baptist Convention Data, Nashville, Tennessee, 2001, www.schoolandstate.org/SBC/Pinckney-WeAreLosingOurChildren.htm.

The Gallup Poll Study, "The Religiosity Cycle," 2002, www.schoolandstate.org/SBC/Pinckney-WeAreLosingOurChildren.htm.

The Southern Baptist Convention's Family Life Council, "Southern Baptist Council on Family Life Report to Annual Meeting of the Southern Baptist Convention," 2002, www.sbcannualmeeting.net/sbc02/newsroom/newspage.asp?ID=261.

Dayton A. Kingsriter, "The Assemblies of God Study," 2007, http://agchurches.org/Sitefiles/Default/RSS/AG%20Colleges/FAQ/Is%20the%20Lower%20Cost%20Worth%20the%20High%20Price_.pdf.

LifeWay Research and Ministry Development, "LifeWay Research Finds Reasons 18- to 22-Year-Olds Drop Out of Church," 2007, www.lifeway.com/ArticleView?storeId=10054&catalogId=10001&langId=-1&article=LifeWay-Research-finds-reasons-18-to-22-year-olds-drop-out-of-church.

George Barna, *Revolution* (BarnaBooks, 2005).

Daniel Cox, Robert P. Jones, and Thomas Banchoff, "A Generation in Transition: Religion, Values, and Politics among College-Age Millennials," Georgetown University's Berkley Center for Religion, Peace, and World Affairs, April 19, 2012, http://publicreligion.org/research/2012/04/millennial-values-survey-2012/#.VgCRYrlRHb0.

Related to the Hostility toward Christianity on College Campuses:

Alexander W. Astin, Helen S. Astin, and Jennifer A. Lindholm, "Spirituality in Higher Education," The Higher Education Research Institute at UCLA, 2010, www.spirituality.ucla.edu/.

Neil Gross and Solon Simmons, "How Religious are America's College and University Professors?," February 6, 2007, http://religion.ssrc.org/reforum/Gross_Simmons.pdf.

4. I excerpted this from Andrew's longer message to me and obtained his approval and permission before copying it here.

CHAPTER 1: DISTINCTIVE DUTY

1. Dietrich Bonhoeffer, *Prisoner for God: Letters and Papers from Prison*, ed. Eberhard Bethge (Minneapolis, MN: Fortress, 1953).

2. William Gurnall, *The Christian in Complete Armour* (Peabody, MA: Hendrickson, 2010).

3. C. S. Lewis, *God in the Dock: Essays on Theology and Ethics* (Grand Rapids, MI: Eerdmans, 1970), 101.

4. *New American Standard Bible*, Matt. 22:37–40 (LaHabra, CA: Lockman, 1995).

5. *New American Standard Bible*, Deut. 6:5 (LaHabra, CA: Lockman, 1995).

6. D. M. Emanuel, "Thinking," *Lexham Theological Wordbook*, ed. D. Mangum, et al. (Bellingham, WA: Lexham, 2014).

7. *New American Standard Bible*, Luke 7:21–23 (LaHabra, CA: Lockman, 1995).

8. *New American Standard Bible*, John 20:24–25 (LaHabra, CA: Lockman, 1995).

9. *New American Standard Bible*, John 20:26–28 (LaHabra, CA: Lockman, 1995).

10. *New American Standard Bible*, John 20:29 (LaHabra, CA: Lockman, 1995).

11. *New American Standard Bible*, John 20:30–31 (LaHabra, CA: Lockman, 1995).

12. Excerpted from the Great Commission passage in Matthew 28:16–20.

13. Papias said the following about Mark's relationship to Peter: "Mark, having become the interpreter of Peter, wrote down accurately, though not indeed in order, whatsoever he remembered of the things said or done by Christ." Papias, quoted in Eusebius, "Church History," *Nicene and Post-Nicene Fathers*, eds. Philip Schaff and Henry Wallace (New York: Cosimo, 2007), 172.

CHAPTER 2: TARGETED TRAINING

1. Origen, as cited in *The Complete Ante-Nicene and Nicene and Post-Nicene Church Fathers Collection*, vol. 9, p. 352.

2. Merriam-Webster online, s.v. "commitment," www.merriam-webster.com/dictionary/commitment.

3. For more information on this survey, see "Barna Survey Examines Changes in Worldview among Christians over the Past Thirteen Years," www.barna.org/barna-update/21-transformation/252-barna-survey-examines-changes-in-worldview-among-christians-over-the-past-13-years#.VjqyKL8hGao, accessed November 4, 2015.

4. For more information on this survey, see "What Do Americans Believe about Jesus? 5 Popular Beliefs," www.barna.org/barna-update/culture/714-what-do-americans-believe-about-jesus-5-popular-beliefs#.VjrAa_-FNhE, accessed November 4, 2015.

5. For more information about the inarticulate nature of young Christians, please refer to Christian Smith and Melinda Lundquist Denton, *Soul Searching: The Religious and Spiritual Lives of American Teenagers* (Oxford: Oxford University Press, April 13, 2009).

6. Dictionary.com, s.v. "train," http://dictionary.reference.com/browse/train?s=t.

7. Visit www.ForensicFaithBook.com to download the assessment test.

8. For more information about this, refer to Christian Smith and Melinda Lundquist Denton, *Soul Searching: The Religious and Spiritual Lives of American Teenagers* (Oxford: Oxford University Press, February 24, 2005).

9. This saying is typically credited to General Abrams, although a precise reference is elusive. See: https://simple.wikiquote.org/wiki/Creighton_Abrams, accessed February 1, 2016.

10. No one leads these missions trips to Utah and the university better than Brett Kunkle. He's the creator of this approach to training. If you'd like him to lead a group for you, contact him through www.str.org.

11. See: https://simple.wikiquote.org/wiki/Creighton_Abrams, accessed February 1, 2016.

CHAPTER 3: INTENSE INVESTIGATION

1. R. C. Sproul, *Knowing Scripture*, ReadHowYouWant, November 11, 2009, p. 7.

2. An excellent example of chronological Bible-reading plans can be found at: www.christianity.com/bible/year/, accessed February 21, 2017.

3. Refer to Gregory Koukl, *Never Read a Bible Verse* (Signal Hill, CA: Stand to Reason, 2000).

4. Papias, quoted in Eusebius, "Church History," *Nicene and Post-Nicene Fathers*, eds. Philip Schaff and Henry Wallace (New York: Cosimo, 2007), 172–73.

5. *New American Standard Bible*, John 21:25 (LaHabra, CA: Lockman, 1995).

6. Luminol is a chemical that reveals the presence of blood, body fluids, or some forms of detergent. These fluids luminesce when exposed to certain forms of light.

7. For a more detailed list related to the statements of Jesus or the evidence demonstrating His deity, please refer to www.ColdCaseChristianity.com.

8. Quoted in *Ante-Nicene Christian Library: Translations of the Writings of the Fathers Down to A.D. 325*, vol. 9, eds. Alexander Roberts and James Donaldson, Irenaeus, Vol. II—Hippolytus, Vol. II—Fragments of Third Century (Edinburgh: T & T Clark, 1870), 188.

9. *Works of Cornelius Tacitus*, includes *Agricola, The Annals, A Dialogue Concerning Oratory, Germania*, and *The Histories* (Boston: MobileReference, 2009), Kindle locations 6393–97.

10. Excerpted from "Letter from Mara Bar-Serapion to His Son," quoted in F. F. Bruce, *The New Testament Documents* (Grand Rapids, MI: Eerdmans, 2011), Kindle locations 1684–88.

11. Quoted in *Ante-Nicene Christian Library*, vol. 9, eds. Roberts and Donaldson, p. 188.

12. See Origen, "Origen against Celsus," *The Ante-Nicene Fathers*, vol. 4, eds. Alexander Roberts and James Donaldson, Tertullian, Part Fourth; Minucius Felix; Commodian; Origen, Parts First and Second (Buffalo: Christian Literature, 1885). Passages cited here are from book 2, chapter 14; book 2, chapter 33; book 2, chapter 59. For more information related to Origen's quotations of Phlegon, refer to www.newadvent.org/fathers/04162 .htm or William Hansen, *Phlegon of Tralles' Book of Marvels* (Exeter, UK: University of Exeter Press, 1997).

13. Refer to the text of M. Schuster as reproduced by W. den Boer, *Scriptorum Paganorum I–IV Saec. de Christianus Testimonia* (Textus Minores 2; rev. ed.; Leiden: Brill, 1965). This version of the text is also cited by Robert E. Van Voorst, *Jesus Outside the New Testament: An Introduction to the Ancient Evidence* (Grand Rapids, MI: Eerdmans, 2000), 25.

14. M. Ihm, ed., C. Suetoni Tranquilli Opera (Teubner Series; Stuttgart: Teubner, 1978) 1:209; Henri Ailloud, ed., Suetone, Vies des douze Cesars (Bude Series; Paris: Societe D'Edition "Les Belles Lettres," 1932) 2:134. For the Teubner text, occasionally altered, with English translation, see J. C. Rolfe, Suetonius (2nd ed; LCL; Cambridge: Harvard University Press, 1997), 2:50–51. This passage is cited, along with a brief discussion related to the validity of the "Christ" reference, in Robert E. Van Voorst, *Jesus Outside the New Testament: An Introduction to the Ancient Evidence* (Grand Rapids, MI: Eerdmans, 2000), 30.

15. From *Against Celsus* 1.28. See Henry Chadwick, *Origen: Contra Celsum* (Cambridge: Cambridge University Press, 1980); and Hoffmann, *Celsus*. Both Borret's Greek text and Chadwick's English translation consider the words I've italicized to belong to Celsus.

16. As I describe in *Cold-Case Christianity* (p. 196), there is controversy about Josephus's writing because early Christians appear to have altered some copies of his work in an effort to amplify the references to Jesus. For this reason, as we examine Josephus's passage related to Jesus, we will rely on a text that scholars believe escaped such alteration, cited from the following source: Shlomo Pines, *An Arabic Version of the Testimonium Flavianum and Its Implications* (Jerusalem: Israel Academy of Sciences and Humanities, 1971), Kindle locations 9–10, 16.

17. b. Sanhedrin 43a, as cited by Robert E. Van Voorst, *Jesus Outside the New Testament: An Introduction to the Ancient Evidence* (Grand Rapids, MI: Eerdmans, 2000), 114.

18. This summary is excerpted from the "Closing Argument" in *God's Crime Scene*. For a much more thorough and detailed examination of the four categories of evidence, including an investigative paradigm to help you make the case to others, please refer to this book.

19. For more information on Christian case maker Frank Turek, please visit www.CrossExamined.org.

20. Ernst Haeckel, "History of Creation," vol. 1, p. 8.

CHAPTER 4: CONVINCING COMMUNICATION

1. Charles F. Stanley, *How to Listen to God* (Nashville, TN: Thomas Nelson, September 1, 2002), chap. 4.

2. William Wilberforce, as quoted by Ron Rhodes in *1001 Unforgettable Quotes about God, Faith, and the Bible* (Eugene, OR: Harvest, April 1, 2011), 20.

3. In the first century, tax collectors like Matthew were typically Jews who worked for the occupying Romans. For this reason, they were seen as traitors. To make matters worse, tax collectors were known to cheat the people they collected from, taking more than they should (as the tax collector Zacchaeus confessed in Luke 19:8).

4. Richard Dawkins, "Has the World Changed?," *The Guardian*, October 11, 2001.

5. Judicial Council of California, "Judicial Council of California Criminal Jury Instructions," CalCrim Section 104.

6. Judicial Council of California, "Judicial Council of California Criminal Jury Instructions," CalCrim Section 103.

7. Luke Muehlhauser, as quoted from his blog post "Atheism and the Burden of Proof," http://commonsenseatheism .com/?p=597, accessed January 12, 2016.

8. Judicial Council of California, "Judicial Council of California Criminal Jury Instructions," CalCrim Section 103.

9. "Clark County Nevada Jury Instructions," NEV. J.I. 1.05, www.clarkcountynv.gov/lawlibrary/Documents /Jury_Instructions.PDF, accessed January 12, 2016.

10. Judicial Council of California, "Judicial Council of California Criminal Jury Instructions," CalCrim Section 105.

11. For more information on this Gallup poll, refer to www.gallup.com/poll/1891/snakes-top-list-americans -fears.aspx, accessed January 12, 2016.

12. James Boccardo, *Unsilenced: How to Voice the Gospel* (CrossBooks, May 20, 2010).

13. J. P. Moreland and William Lane Craig, *Philosophical Foundations for a Christian Worldview* (Downers Grove, IL: IVP Academic, April 28, 2003), 30.

14. Harry Elmer Barnes, *An Intellectual and Cultural History of the Western World* (Mineola, NY: Dover, 1965), 766, quoted from Albert J. Menendez and Edd Doerr, *The Great Quotations on Religious Freedom.*

REBUTTAL NOTES

1. Dictionary.com, s.v. "tolerance," http://dictionary.reference.com/browse/tolerance, accessed January 21, 2016.

THE MOST IMPORTANT CASE OF YOUR LIFE

Through the *Forensic Faith Curriculum Kit,* cold-case homicide detective **J. Warner Wallace** shows us why it's important to develop a forensic faith and how to become effective Christian case makers.

This eight-week program will help you
- understand why we have a duty to defend the truth;
- develop a training strategy to master the evidence for Christianity;
- learn how to employ the techniques of a detective to discover new insights from God's Word; and
- become better communicators by learning the skills of professional case makers.

Using real-life detective stories, fascinating strategies, biblical insights, and his own visual illustrations, Wallace shares cold-case investigative disciplines we can apply to our Christian faith.

   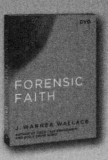

Available in print and digital editions
everywhere books are sold

transforming lives together

IT'S TIME FOR A "COLD-CASE" APPROACH TO THE GOSPELS

A cold-case homicide detective takes the lessons he has learned from years of investigation and uses them to examine the evidence, eyewitnesses, and records of the New Testament. Can the Gospels be trusted despite the evidence or because of it?

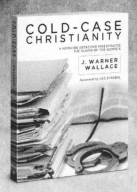

"*Cold-Case Christianity* is a fantastic book. I wish I had this resource when I first examined the Christian faith. It would have answered many of my questions and helped set me on the track to truth."

—Josh McDowell,
speaker and author of
Evidence That Demands a Verdict

Available in print and digital editions
everywhere books are sold

David C Cook
transforming lives together

COULD THE UNIVERSE JUST HAPPEN?
THE EVIDENCE WILL REVEAL THE TRUTH

A former atheist and seasoned cold-case detective invites readers to sit on the jury as he makes a compelling case for God's existence with eight critical pieces of evidence found in the crime scene of our universe.

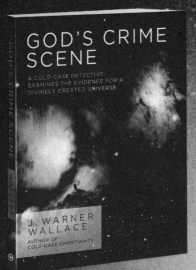

"Around *Dateline,* we had a phrase to describe J. Warner Wallace: 'The Evidence Whisperer.'"

—Keith Morrison,
news correspondent with *Dateline NBC*

"Imagine a crime scene as big as ... the entire universe! That's what cold-case homicide detective J. Warner Wallace does in this compelling and creative book as he shows how the evidence points powerfully toward a Creator."

—Lee Strobel,
New York Times bestselling author and professor at Houston Baptist University

Available in print and digital editions everywhere books are sold

David C Cook
transforming lives together